Unconditional

Love and Life with Greyhounds

Jeanne Cassidy

UNCONDITIONAL
LOVE AND LIFE WITH GREYHOUNDS

Copyright © 2021 Jeanne Cassidy.

All rights reserved. No part of this book may be used or reproduced by any means, graphic, electronic, or mechanical, including photocopying, recording, taping or by any information storage retrieval system without the written permission of the author except in the case of brief quotations embodied in critical articles and reviews.

iUniverse books may be ordered through booksellers or by contacting:

iUniverse
1663 Liberty Drive
Bloomington, IN 47403
www.iuniverse.com
844-349-9409

Because of the dynamic nature of the Internet, any web addresses or links contained in this book may have changed since publication and may no longer be valid. The views expressed in this work are solely those of the author and do not necessarily reflect the views of the publisher, and the publisher hereby disclaims any responsibility for them.

Any people depicted in stock imagery provided by Getty Images are models, and such images are being used for illustrative purposes only.
Certain stock imagery © Getty Images.

ISBN: 978-1-6632-3338-7 (sc)
ISBN: 978-1-6632-3339-4 (e)

Library of Congress Control Number: 2021924921

Print information available on the last page.

iUniverse rev. date: 12/08/2021

1-17-22

Dear Dorothea —

Thank you for your friendship and kindness! It's been lovely to know you and dear Honey!

With love —
Jean Cassidy

To all who help animals

Contents

Acknowledgments xi

Chapter 1	A Morning in the Early 1990s 1
Chapter 2	Our First: Ping Ping 3
Chapter 3	Tootsie 21
Chapter 4	A Day Like No Other 27
Chapter 5	The Order of Life: Change 39
Chapter 6	Celia 45
Chapter 7	Tootsie and Miss Daisy 53
Chapter 8	Miss Daisy 63
Chapter 9	Sophie and Dora 69
Chapter 10	And Then Came Darby 71
Chapter 11	Road Trip 77
Chapter 12	More Change 83
Chapter 13	Eileen 85

Afterword 89
About the Author 91
Bibliography 93

They run for their lives
Winning money for their owners
And those who gamble with tens and fives.
With streamlined bodies and muscular hips,
Soft brown eyes and long snouts,
with sensitive noses at the tips,
They run for their lives.
Black, fawn, white, and grey,
Some colors mixed with others,
Historically gentle, with good sight for prey,
In Europe only the wealthy could own them,
Forbidden to anyone else—
In Egypt, second only to a pharaoh's son.
They run for their lives,
Held in cages, fed from troughs,
Racing their hearts till they're worn.
When time on the track for them is done,
Owners release them as though they weren't born.
No longer running for their lives
And trucking from track to track,
They met unspeakable ends,
Until their stories were told
And heeded by those who'd be friends.
The truth did make them free
And able to live to be old.
Now animal lovers work hard
To find these innocents homes
Where they can frolic in a yard
And gratefully lie on soft beds
As precious companions and friends.
—Jeanne Cassidy, 2017

acknowledgments

My great thanks go to:

- Eileen McCaughern, one of my heroes, and animal advocates everywhere
- Alan Mindell who encouraged me to continue my writing
- Irene Brennan, my dear friend who helped with proofing, editing, and encouragement
- Mikey Urell, my nephew who helped with photos and suggestions
- Michelle Skaar, who took time to help me with format issues
- Kristen Jensen, who took the beautiful portraits of Tootsie and of Daisy
- Tom, my husband, and my sons, Tom and John, for their patience and support
- Everyone at iUniverse
- And all who helped me to take good care of all the girls.

Chapter 1

A Morning in the Early 1990s

"ARE YOU WATCHING JOAN RIVERS?" ASKED MY HUSBAND, calling me at my office.

I wasn't, so I switched in time to see a sandy-colored dog licking Joan's cheek. A woman from REGAPCT (Retired Greyhounds as Pets, Connecticut), Eileen McCaughern, had brought several of these beautiful hounds to *The Joan Rivers Show*, which aired in New York City from 1989 through 1993 and garnered an Emmy Award for its host.

"Can we get one?" Tom asked. "There's a number to call."

"Will you have time to take care of a pet?" I asked. "It will need to walk several times each day, and we live in the city. What happens when you travel—and what about our cat?"

"They are beautiful dogs," he countered. "I've never seen one up close before! They seem so gentle and sweet! I don't think they would bother Elizabeth. Why don't I call and get more information?"

"Good idea," I replied. I loved what I saw on screen. I'd always heard and sometimes seen that large dogs were calmer than small ones. Greyhounds seemed to be gentle and affectionate.

My work was busy, so I filed the thought for further consideration. They were lovely, friendly dogs who needed homes. I knew that Tom would make the call, and I was excited to hear more.

1

Chapter 2

Our First: Ping Ping

Jeanne, Ping Ping, and Tom enjoying a Greyhound picnic at Riverside Park in Manhattan in the early nineties

B ARKING, WHINING, AND SOUNDS OF RATTLING CRATES FILLED the air as tears filled my eyes. They knew why we were here. More than thirty of them lived in the basement of this home in South Windsor, Connecticut—male, female, beige, black, brindle, white, and combinations. Some had come directly from a track. Others had been returned due to family problems or other situations. The sounds and sights were overwhelming. How could we possibly make a choice?

Tom's call had been received by a Mr. Botticello, who called to give us directions to his home in Connecticut where he housed hounds retired from the nearby Plainfield Track. He had been affiliated with the track at one time and, after retiring, opened his heart to help REGAP find homes for the retired hounds. When Eileen McCaughern had established REGAPCT the two joined forces and worked together for many years. This kind man had converted his basement into a kennel and his backyard into paths of runs for the dogs' exercise. He had retired from the Hartford Civic Center where he had been Maintenance Supervisor. Mr. Botticello and his sons had bred and raced greyhounds who were winners at several tracks on the East Coast. Unlike many owners and breeders at this time this kind man wanted the hounds to live happily for the rest of their lives.

To help with our choice, Mr. Botticello took us into a small back room where a few crates stood against the back wall. Directing us to the first, he introduced us to a quiet, sandy-colored female who was cringing at the back of her crate. She was only two years old.

"Avonlea is her name," he said. "She wasn't fast enough to stay on the track for very long."

He brought another dog over in order to encourage Avonlea to come out and be close to us. We spoke softly to her and held out our hands for sniffing. Mr. Santoro leashed her. "Why don't you take her for a walk outside?" he suggested.

I hadn't walked a dog for many years, but Avonlea seemed fine and easily followed along. I was the one who was nervous. Since our apartment was small and on the fifteenth floor of a large building in a busy neighborhood, a quiet and calm dog seemed perfect for us. The walking area was clean and cared for, with a number of walkways for the dogs to use for exercise. Avonlea walked calmly by my side, and I was confident that I could handle this.

All was going well until a thought occurred to me: we had forgotten about Elizabeth, our cat, who had been queen of the house until now.

She disliked car travel intensely, so we usually left her in New York unless we would be spending more than just the weekend in Connecticut. Getting her into the carrier took two of us about half an hour.

So Elizabeth was in New York and had not been informed that we were adopting a greyhound with whom she would have to share her space. Another challenge to meet! *It shouldn't be too difficult,* I assured myself. *Both animals are docile beings, and we'll be careful and watchful. We'll make it work.*

We decided to change our new girl's name from Avonlea to Ping Ping, a name Tom brought back from China where he traveled yearly to represent a great many international publishers. Books written in English were in great demand at universities there. One of the Chinese women who worked with him was named Ping Ping. After growing up with two brothers and living with my husband and two sons for the past years, I was determined to have some female company in addition to Elizabeth in our household.

Mr. Botticello gave us food recommendations, a muzzle, and a folded crate to help with introductions at home, and he assured us that we could return Ping Ping if things didn't work out. We had to promise never to race her and to have her spayed. In addition, he gave us the name and address of Eileen McCaughern, the REGAPCT person we had seen on Joan Rivers' show. Her home in Bethany, Connecticut, was not far from ours in Litchfield County

Before we left, we made a donation to help support all the other hounds. It was sad to leave them, and we hoped that other dog lovers had seen the show and would call as we did.

Our hearts raced as we took Ping Ping to our car, where she lay down in the back while we loaded her accessories. As we drove north to Torrington, we spoke softly, using her new name over and over. Next stop was the pet store. Dishes, food, a leash, and a soft bed filled the bill.

★ ★ ★

Our home was in the foothills of the Berkshire Mountains in a recreational community that attracted many New Yorkers like us for weekend retreats. When we got home, we took a quick walk before entering our condo. We lived on a lovely and peaceful street nestled in the woods, not far from a stable and a dog run. Ping availed herself of the space and walked briskly back to the house with me.

The house had two floors filled with sunlight and several beds and couches—perfect for "couch potatoes," another name for retired Greyhounds. We placed Ping's bowls on a mat. She took a long drink of fresh water and followed us on a tour upstairs and down. We fed her and ourselves, watched some TV with Ping lying near us on the carpet, and then took a pre-bedtime walk.

"Where's the best place for her to sleep?" I wondered.

"How about putting her mat in the guest bathroom?" Tom suggested. "It's small and nearby so that we can hear her if she barks."

It was a good solution. Our sleep was uninterrupted and, thankfully, sound until daybreak.

"Let's see how Ping Ping is … Oh my gosh! She's in the bathtub—not on her soft, comfortable mat! How did that happen? She must have felt safer in an enclosed place—like her crate!"

"I hope she wasn't cold," said Tom. "When we get back to New York, we'll set up her crate, and she'll spend her nights there for a while."

We lifted the dog out of the slippery tub and got ready for a walk and breakfast.

It was a lovely spring morning as we walked out toward the stable. Ping's ears were up, and she was smiling. (Dogs do smile.) She had a very long tongue, I thought, but I hadn't seen very many greyhounds before. Perhaps they all had long tongues.

A group of pet owners in our community had raised money for a well-appointed dog run next to the garden area at the stable. After a brisk walk, we sat on a bench with our morning coffee, watching Ping

Ping and the other dogs enjoy their freedom. It was a great way to start the day. Next, a tour of the barn and the surroundings led us to chickens, goats, cats, and a pig. Horses were grazing in several fenced areas. They acknowledged us with neighs. The goats looked for treats, the chickens clucked, and the cats disappeared as we approached. The pig was quiet and depressed. She had been a house pet previously. Ping took all we saw in stride.

After lunch, we went to the sports field, where there was a baseball diamond in front of us. We unleashed Ping, and to our surprise and delight, she ran the bases as though the diamond was a racetrack. It must have resembled a track or a run she had experienced. Her strides and speed were a joy to behold for those, like us, who had never closely watched greyhounds run. Their bodies were designed for speed like a sports car, it seemed. She smiled when she reached the finish line, and so did we.

★ ★ ★

Weekends are always too short. Soon we had to take the long ride back to the city. On the way, we made one stop for Ping, and we discussed how to prepare for our arrival at the apartment, where Elizabeth awaited our return. First, we'd take a walk around the city block—a big change from the countryside we had left. We would make sure to have Ping muzzled, just in case.

It was autumn of 1990. We lived in an historic building in Chelsea, in Manhattan, called London Towers. The view from our fifteenth-floor home was of the Hudson River. Many famous and interesting people had, and still did, live there: writers, photographers, artists, actors, etc. The Olympic-sized pool downstairs had held Billy Rose's rehearsals for aquacades—such great history!

It was a pet-friendly environment—birds, dogs, cats. The neighborhood was diverse and included many gay people. Shops and restaurants abounded, along with two movie theaters. The subway and buses were nearby, and it was a short walk to the waterfront.

As we opened the door to the apartment with Ping Ping in tow, a blur of white streaked across the living room and settled under a table near the windows.

"Hi, Elizabeth," I said. "This is your new sister, Ping Ping."

A muzzled Ping made her way to the table, sniffed the furry blur, and was greeted with a paw to her nose. No further introductions seemed necessary.

Setting up the crate was a priority. As soon as we had placed the soft mat inside, Ping went in and lay down. Our kitchen was small, but we found a separate area for Ping's bowls far from Elizabeth's place under the window. As we showed Ping around the apartment, we assured her that she and Elizabeth would become good friends.

★ ★ ★

Before long, we had a routine going. First thing each morning, I walked and fed Ping, took a swim, and went off to work—all before eight o'clock. How did we do it? Volume![1] We were always busy and always found time for fun. All the while, from under her table, Elizabeth watched all activity in the household. Her vigilance sharpened when Ping began to venture out of her crate, which was left open and available for emergencies during the day.

Soon, we left the door to the crate open in the evening. Next, we allowed Ping to sleep on her mat in our bedroom. Of course, one night she happened to jump into our king-size bed, and that was the end of the floor mat, never mind the crate.

I wish I had taken a photo the morning I walked into the kitchen and spotted Elizabeth in Ping's crate. It was a wonderful first laugh of my day!

---

[1] Borrowed from a comedy routine by Robert Klein.

"Hi, Elizabeth, how is it in there?" I asked.

She looked up at me with her soft brown eyes and meowed. She looked happy and comfortable. Had I closed the door, she might have freaked out. So I just let her enjoy herself where she was.

For a while, I thought the two girls pretty much ignored each other. Imagine my surprise and relief when I came home one day to find them lying on the couch together, but not *too* together.

★ ★ ★

When Tom and I traveled, our superintendent's wife would come to care for our pets. Following a week's business trip, we came home and were shocked to find Ping with a big plastic collar around her neck and a reddish rash on her hindquarters. What could have happened while we were gone? Mrs. Sullivan had taken her to the vet, who had prescribed meds but had not found a reason for the rash. The salve the doctor prescribed seemed to be helping very little, at least so far.

We were planning to attend a Madison Square Garden greyhound event on the following Saturday with Ping in tow. So many beautiful hounds in one place, with vendors for pet food and supplies everywhere! One person from a food company stopped by our area and noticed the rash. He convinced us that his brand might be helpful. Combined with the salve and an antibiotic, the new diet did clear up the rash in a few weeks.

Not long after the Garden event, there was a Greyhound picnic scheduled in a park uptown. It was wonderful to see so many hounds who lived in Manhattan. Though Ping was still very shy and not a joiner, we had fun and made good friends with Amy and her hound, Patches. Amy had adopted Patches and, best of all, she owned a wonderful pet store in our neighborhood. Patches and Ping Ping became good friends too.

★ ★ ★

I was scheduled for some surgery a few months later and was released to go home in the early evening of the same day. I asked Tom to sleep in the living room with the pets that night, and until I felt better. At midnight, I heard a knock at the door, accompanied by much begging and pleading. Ping and Tom had been nudging each other off the couch throughout the evening so that neither could sleep. So we stuffed pillows between all of us and slept together soundly until morning.

All the while, Ping and Elizabeth had been getting more and more comfortable with each other. It was easier for us to leave for an evening knowing that they kept each other company. Elizabeth was nearly twenty years old. Though she looked and behaved OK, she did seem to be slowing down and not eating as much as usual. Time for a visit to Dr. Marcos.

Dr. Marcos diagnosed her with cancer and suggested that we spend precious time with her for a while and then schedule a date for her passing. Her slowing down had been gradual, and she didn't seem to be in pain, but how could we know? Pets can't tell us how they feel. We have to pay close attention to their behavior. We would sadly heed Dr. Marcos's advice.

New York City has many interesting neighborhoods. Ours was Chelsea—crowded and friendly and filled with interesting people. A retired man who lived close to the vet's office visited there each day without fail. He had met Elizabeth when she boarded there a few times. He had heard that she would be leaving us on the day we chose. When we arrived at the office on that day, there was a white rose on the counter left for Elizabeth by the kind man. New York, New York, a heck of a town, filled with good souls with good hearts. We would find them wherever we went.

Elizabeth had come to us from a backyard in Brooklyn. Some thought she was a doorstop, as she lay quietly under her table most of the time. To the end, she fought for her life. She gave us many years of love—Elizabeth, our special calico cat.

★ ★ ★

A few blocks from our building, there was a large park used for neighborhood basketball and baseball games. Early one Saturday morning, we walked over to let Ping have some running space that she hadn't had since our weekends in Connecticut. We unleashed her and let her run back and forth to and from us.

The second time around, she ran right past me to the open park gate and into the thankfully empty street. How could I have forgotten that all of this was new to her, that she had had few opportunities to run freely, let alone in a big city with endless cars, trucks, buses, and people? Should I run after her? *No!* Should I yell? *No!*

"Ping," I called gently and calmly as I crouched down and offered a treat in my outstretched hand. She stopped and seemed to give thought to her next move. I continued to speak softly and hold out the cookie as my heart pounded. She came closer and at last accepted the offer. "Good girl!"

After hugs and pats, I was able to leash her and choose a safer corner of the park in which to play. A lesson to remember: be aware of what could possibly happen in a new environment, especially with a new pet.

Due to busy schedules, we took Ping to doggy daycare in midtown one morning. Upon our return, we found that she had suffered a wound and been stitched. The owner gave no plausible explanation for what had happened.

We asked for the name of the veterinarian and called. He told us that Ping had been bitten by another dog. We were very disappointed that the owner had not been honest with us. From then on, we chose to use individual dog sitters when we needed them.

Buster was a purebred Boston bulldog owned by two friends in our building. One of them was quite ill and asked Tom to walk Buster each day at lunchtime. He and Tom were two of several residents who worked at home.

It was impossible to walk Ping and Buster together. Buster was pokey and slow, while Ping trotted along briskly. So Tom got lots of exercise in all kinds of weather.

Ping had a winter coat and a raincoat. Buster had a wardrobe that included a black leather jacket and hat along with other outfits. Their competition was two Italian greyhounds who wore matching sweaters designed by their owner and a white standard poodle from the next block who wore pearls each day. The charm of Chelsea was, and is, its diversity.

★ ★ ★

Though we loved our Chelsea neighborhood, we decided to sell our place while the real estate market was doing well. It was the nineties. Renting rather than owning until our retirement became our plan. We would buy again in the future when we found a place in Connecticut for the next stage of our lives.

We noticed that there were several new buildings advertised in Battery Park City. Soon after that, Tom called me at work to say that he had found a great new building located right next to the Hudson River. It had more space, a beautiful view, the neighborhood was "up and coming," and there was a dog run right across the street—perfect for all of us! Best of all, when we listed our Chelsea apartment for sale, we found that our neighbor who lived on the floor directly beneath us wanted to make a duplex and had received permission to do so. How perfect for all concerned!

Moving has always been an adventure for me. I love space-planning and decorating—getting a new start! Our new home was called Riverwatch, and our view across the river included the Statue of Liberty and Ellis Island. Our new area had been built on landfill, and the buildings included the World Trade Center, a shopping area, other apartments, a beautiful walkway, and a wonderful museum next door. There was an office for Tom and floor-to-ceiling living room windows where Ping loved to hang out. It was all we needed and more—almost another world attached to Manhattan.

As soon as we were somewhat settled, friends and designers Wing Kee and Bruce come to visit and help hang artwork. It was cocktail hour with drinks and cheeses on the coffee table. When we finished, we set out to hang pictures in suitable areas. When we returned to the living room, a very large wheel of cheese had disappeared from the table. Guess who?

Though the cheese was not harmful, the size of the wheel was concerning. But Ping was fine the next morning, and I learned not to leave food on a low table. Thank goodness she had not sampled the drinks!

The evening was otherwise a great success. Bruce and Wing Kee did a fabulous job. They had learned a lesson years before when they had a black cat they forgot about when they decorated their apartment all in black. When finding the cat became a challenge, redecoration became necessary!

Of course, the dog run was Ping's favorite part of our new neighborhood. Soon after the move-in, she and I met Diane and her little terrier, Lucy. Lucy chased a tennis ball endlessly between five and five thirty each morning. Diane and I were office early birds—she in a financial firm in Battery Park, myself at MTV-Music Television at Times Square. We became fast friends. In summer, fall, winter, and spring, what might have seemed a chore was another wonderful part of living in this lovely area.

Ping had no interest in chasing a ball. She did seem to like the soft toy animals we bought at the pet store. She carried them from place to place but never chewed them up. They were her companions in her bed or on the couch or on our bed.

Rarely were Ping and I alone in the dog run, but one spring day Lucy and Diane did not appear. It was sunny and quiet as I sat watching Ping and enjoying the peace. I had brought a brush to groom her winter fur now that the weather was warming. From the trees surrounding the run, birds seemed to be chirping louder than usual.

Ping moved closer, reminding me that time was short. I looked up and saw that the birds were flying in and out of the run to pick up the fur on the pavement. It must have made their nests so soft for the eggs they would lay there soon. Another happy morning!

On the way to work, I was reminded of a time in my youth. I was probably twelve and very concerned with my hairstyle. In fact, I was trimming it now and then. I knew that my mother would be upset to know this. I must have thought if I threw the cuttings out the window, she would never know what I was doing.

Much to my surprise, one spring day Mom asked whether I was cutting my hair. I lied, saying "No."

She answered, "Come with me."

She led me outside to a hedge next to our driveway, and there was a bird's nest lined with my hair! We had to laugh together. Lucky for me that it was a laugh.

★ ★ ★

Our new life in Battery Park City continued happily. When Tom traveled twice each year to China, Ping and I were fine. Linda, Tom's efficient and responsible assistant, spent each weekday in Tom's office and walked Ping while I was working.

I loved my job. The hours were long and busy. Most of my coworkers were under forty. I wasn't, but I felt like it when I was there. It was MTV, a new, exciting, and successful cable channel.

And best of all, I went home to Battery Park City each day and was met at the door with a smile and a wagging tail. Weekends were spent with friends and trips to movies, museums, concerts, and art galleries There was extra time to spend with Ping just enjoying our neighborhood together.

One summer, we rented out our second home in Connecticut, where we usually spent weekends and holidays, and chose to spend a glorious two months in the city. In summer, many New Yorkers spent weekends elsewhere, so it was easier to get around and enjoy places that were less crowded. Then, in August, Tom took his autumn trip to the Beijing Bookfair in China. After our tenants had left our house, Ping and I drove up to Connecticut to get the house back together—not the best way to spend a weekend, but still a nice change. We spent the night and left the house in good order in the morning, hoping to beat the Sunday traffic. Ping spread out on the back seat for a nap, and we began a peaceful drive back to Manhattan.

When we got to the West Side Highway, traffic was heavy and bumper-to-bumper. As we were passing the cruise-ship docks, I looked to see what ships were docked and didn't see how close I was to a very beat-up red car in front of me. I heard a tapping sound. The red car stopped and the driver jumped out to tell me that I had hit his car.

I suggested that we enter the parking lot nearby. "Don't you see the license plate?" he asked. "My passenger is handicapped!"

I had locked my doors and opened my window halfway. "I'm so sorry! Shall I call the police?"

"No" was his answer. Then he noticed my backseat passenger with her ears perked. Ping was shy but large. The driver had to agree with me that the "dent" was hard to find and barely visible.

"I have forty dollars. Will that take care of it?" I asked.

He agreed, keeping an eye on the back seat. We settled, and I breathed a long sigh of relief driving the rest of the way to the parking garage, keeping my eyes sharply on the road. "Thanks, Ping! But for you it might have been much worse!" She smiled and lowered her ears.

★ ★ ★

When Tom returned that fall, I suggested that we visit my brother Jim in West Virginia. He had invited us and said we could bring Ping along. He had a wonderful black lab named Ruff, a cat named Ethel (after our mom), and several horses bred for racing at the local track.

One of his daughters and her husband had helped him with his introduction to horse racing. Knowing how beautiful the Blue Ridge Mountains were said to be, we were very happy to be invited. We started out early in the morning, and we were able to reach his home by late afternoon the same day.

Ping and Ruff were fine together as we toured Jim's rented farm. The place was lovely. As we walked, Jim pointed out a corral where a bay mare in foal stood by herself. Ping trotted over and tucked herself under the fence. To our surprise, she and the mare began to frolic together and trotted around for a while as a mother and foal might do. What a touching sight!

Next to greyhounds, horses are my favorite animals. I treasure having had them in my life. It was a wonderful weekend and so worth the long and lovely drive. It warmed my heart to see my brother and his animals so well and happy.

★ ★ ★

Back in New York, our good life continued. Ping and Lucy played together each morning as Diane and I solved the world's problems. New York City was the best place we could be! On my way home, I could meet Tom at the Downtown Athletic Club for a swim in their Olympic-sized pool and then have dinner in their bar and restaurant. This building housed apartments where many young, unmarried men who worked in the Financial Center lived. And all of this across the highway from Battery Park City!

Whatever the season, wonders never ceased. I've always enjoyed all four of the seasons. Each one brings its own beauty. Fall is my favorite because leaves turn such beautiful colors and school starts. Snow in the country seemed softer and easier to manage. Dogs become friskier at play in the snow. In the city, piles of snow from the plows often block parking places and parts of sidewalks, but there are Christmas and Hanukkah and New Year celebrations to enjoy. Spring brings new life and flowers and relief from heavy clothes and boots. Summer has a slowdown in pace and more fun outdoors. One learns to adjust for each and to appreciate all the differences.

One winter morning, I dressed Ping and myself warmly for the cold. "Oh, Ping! It's been snowing, and it's still really coming down!"

Looking toward the river, we watched the QE2 quietly sailing through the snowflakes into the harbor, visible only by its running lights. The sight was magical and breathtaking at the same time. Thoughts of the history of that vessel came to me, and my mind's eye stores the memory of that morning still.

In our living room, the floor-to-ceiling windows overlooked the Hudson River. Ping had a favorite corner where she could view all the activity and enjoy the sun. Otherwise, she lay on one of the sectionals or on the sofa in Tom's office. Ping was the only one of our hounds who sometimes slept in what I called the "dead roach position"—on her back with her legs in the air. The living room sectional provided the perfect place for her to take that pose. Whenever she could, she would be where one or both of us were.

★ ★ ★

Time goes too quickly in the lives of dogs. I noticed that Ping seemed to be slowing down and was not as energetic as before. Tom was in China at the time. I made an appointment for a checkup with our veterinarian back in Chelsea and planned for a day off from work. Dr. Johnson examined her and recommended that I take her to the New York Animal Hospital uptown. Ping was almost eleven, a good age for a large dog, especially one who had been on the track.

A week later, the hospital doctor informed me that Ping's heart was enlarged and gave me medication to give her at home. For nearly a week, she was OK, and then she began to show additional symptoms. She spent a few more days in the hospital, and I visited her each day. They had a quiet space where we could sit on the floor together. It was hard to go home without her. After getting meds updated, I was able to take her home once again a few days later. Thank goodness!

Tom called from China each day, but I made no mention of Ping's condition. "We're all just fine!" I would say. He would have worried and couldn't do anything to help. He would be there for three weeks.

Soon, Ping began spending a lot of time in one of our bathrooms, where it was dark and quiet. She didn't whine or moan and continued to eat most of her food, but her energy level seemed lower each day. I called the hospital and was told that they could not increase her meds any further.

When I called Dr. Johnson, our vet, he suggested that Ping's life had been long and that her time might be near, and I should consider putting her to sleep. I didn't want to think about what I should do, so I filed it in the back of my mind. Every walk we took became precious. Every morning spent in the run, watching the boats on the river together, meeting other dogs … all seemed so special because we could be close.

It was hard to keep my secret from Tom. I talked with Ping about all our happy times together. I called my best friend, Sue, who cherished her dogs and cats, and we wept together. Lizanne, my great New York City friend, invited me to dinner, where we both talked about our pets.

Sadly, she had recently lost her cat. Our pets mean so much to us! It doesn't seem fair that their lives are so much shorter than ours.

As Ping grew more listless, spending more time in the dark bathroom, reality came to the fore. I had to do this. I called Dr. Johnson's office and made an appointment for a midmorning early in the next week. Linda agreed to go with us. I told my office that I would be off that day, and for the next few days I made the most of my time left with Ping.

Early on the day of the appointment, Ping and I went for a long slow walk along the river. We listened to the birds, heard the lapping of the water against the pilings, felt the fresh morning air, and watched the tugboats and ferries doing their jobs. We sat and talked about the times we had enjoyed together. Her perked ears told me that she was listening. "It has been so lovely to know and love you, Ping. You taught me so much that I hadn't fully realized before: unconditional love, simple pleasures, patience, forgiveness." We spent as much time as we could next to the river in our favorite place.

Back at the apartment, we were just in time for Linda to arrive. I told her we would leave in half an hour. Ping drank some water from her dish and began to walk through the apartment, ending up at the window in her favorite corner. Was she looking for Tom? Was she saying goodbye? Did she know that this day was her last?

I called for a pet taxi so that we could all be comfortable. It came too soon. A friendly, and soft-spoken young driver met us outside. He asked why we were going to the vet. When I told him, he opened his lunch bag and shared his roast beef sandwich with Ping. She loved it.

I explained how we had come to this decision, that she had been treated but kept losing strength, and that she had spent much time in the dark bathroom. He shared with us that finding dogs in bathrooms in the city was common. It seemed to be a safe and quiet retreat for them. I remembered Ping's first night with us, sleeping in the bathtub in Connecticut nine years before. It didn't seem as funny now. Her time with us had been too short.

Too soon, we arrived at the vet's office, where we were ushered into a quiet white room with bare walls, sparsely furnished with a table, where we had a few minutes to say our goodbyes. My tears never stopped as I told Ping how much we loved her and would miss her. Too soon, the doctor and an aide came in and lifted her onto the table with kind and gentle hands. Linda and I repeated our loving goodbyes and hugs as she passed peacefully. Dear Ping, our beautiful hound—you brought so much joy to our lives.

A week later, Tom arrived home, asking for Ping the moment I opened the front door. I couldn't put what had happened into words. My tears told the story. The two of us sobbed through the night. Our hearts were broken. Our sweet and gentle Ping—a life too short. It was March 2001.

Chapter 3

Tootsie

Tootsie, a black beauty

IT WAS A QUIET SATURDAY MORNING. WE WERE TAKING OUR TIME with coffee while enjoying our view of the river—such a relief after a busy week. All of Ping's belongings remained under the dining table where I had placed them after she left us. It had been almost two months since her passing.

We had sold our Connecticut house. It was a great community and could be our retirement home someday. Right now, though, New

York was such a perfect place for us—theatre, museums, art galleries, wonderful restaurants, concerts, and cultural events were more than enough to fill our days and nights. One home to manage was enough for us at this point. Our careers kept us very busy, and the other house required attention we had little time to give.

"Remember all those dogs in Mr. Botticello's basement?" I asked Tom. "Can we think about bringing another greyhound home? Yes, they break your heart when they leave, but life is like that."

Tom needed to give it some thought. We had loved Ping Ping's companionship so much. Did we want our hearts broken once again?

Following the next work week, we spoke again, and this time, Tom agreed that other dogs needed loving homes. "Let's call Eileen at REGAPCT and let her know that we have room in our hearts for another hound!" he said.

★ ★ ★

Eileen was thrilled to hear from us. "Come up this weekend!" she said. "I have some new hounds. I have several females you might like."

And so, we drove to Bethany on a Saturday morning in the summer. Bethany was a quiet Connecticut community of homes and small businesses. There were a number of farms with horse-loving people there also. Eileen's home was on two acres with a heated barn for a retired horse she had acquired. Not far away, in Naugatuck, was the Peter Paul Mounds factory. It was fun driving by as we headed for Eileen's place. The scent of chocolate filled the air for blocks!

At least fifteen dogs were in a large, fenced area behind Eileen's house. As we pulled into the driveway, we could hear barking and whining. They heard us! Eileen waved us in. It was great to see her and the hounds in person after watching them on *The Joan Rivers Show*.

Right away, Eileen introduced us to a playful black female with white markings on her chest and paws. She had won some races in Massachusetts the previous season. "She seems friendly," I said, "and I love her markings: white paws and a white chest and such a shiny black coat—so beautiful." And she was smiling! The other hounds gathered together behind the fence, whining and leaping up toward us, begging to be noticed. There were so many choices, and the dogs all knew why we were there. They were all beautiful! I wished we could take more than one.

It was our first opportunity to meet Eileen, who seemed to be such a special person. She had done this work for many years and waited patiently for us to choose our new companion. We had brought a collar and a leash, certain that we would take a hound home that day.

And so we chose our next companion: black and beautiful! Although her track name had been Windborne, I favored the name Tootsie, inspired by my favorite film, *Tootsie* with Dustin Hoffman. His portrayal of a woman with great spirit and grit inspired me to choose a dog with spirit and grit, which Windborne surely seemed to be.

We did the paperwork and gave a donation to Eileen to support her work. We leashed Tootsie, and when Tom began to lead her to the car, she leaped about three feet into the air, nearly taking Tom with her. *What fun*, I thought.

Eileen reminded us that we could board Tootsie with her whenever we had to travel. And, of course, if there were problems (maybe too much spirit), we could bring her back to Bethany. Good to know!

We drove straight back to New York with a happy hound in the back seat. She smiled all the way. When we arrived, the first stop was the dog run across the street from our building. A few other dogs were there. They sniffed Tootsie and walked away. Good sign!

When I opened our apartment door, Tom disconnected the leash, and Tootsie leaped over the couch and into the living room, smiling as she flew. Life was going to be interesting, hopefully fun, and certainly different from our years with Ping.

★ ★ ★

Very quickly, Tootsie adapted to her new life. She loved all the soft places to lie, the private meals, and the toys we had saved that had been Ping's. She was a bit more aggressive with the toys than Ping had been, but she never chewed them up.

She was comfortable in our New York neighborhood, Battery Park City. Tom's office was in our apartment, and his secretary, Linda, worked with him each day. So, during the week, Toots was never alone unless Tom and I went out for an evening. However, on weekends, we sometimes left her alone for a while to join an activity or to shop uptown.

As our neighbors learned that we had a new hound, they realized that sounds they had thought were fire engines or ambulances sometimes were actually Tootsie's cries while we were out. After a while, we noticed that much of the frame around the front door had been chewed. Time for a checkup!

Racing greyhounds are never alone. Their crates are lined up all together in large rooms. They run on tracks together. They share troughs of food and water. No wonder Toots was lonely! Our veterinarian diagnosed her with separation anxiety. What to do? Toots could not bear to be alone. Although toys, food, water, and soft couches were always available, they were not enough. Toots needed other beings with her. Another hound would be too hard to handle in our New York apartment A good solution might be a pet sitter.

Dog walkers (and sitters) make a good living in New York, where persons can walk several dogs at a time in residential areas. One could easily find an apartment sitter and/or a pet sitter in the city. It was a great job for students or those who enjoyed part-time work.

And so, Anita came into our lives. "Thanks for coming, Anita! Thanks for answering our call. We heard about you from friends. This is Tootsie. I'll show you around our place and then we can take her for a walk."

Hearing the word *walk*, Tootsie wagged her tail and smiled. Anita laughed and greeted her with a smile and a pat. The two seemed comfortable with each other as we toured our space and then walked the path along the Hudson together. Anita was able to hold the leash and Toots with ease. Problem solved: Anita agreed to be available when we needed her. Hooray!

Each morning, I was up and dressed by five o'clock so I could take Tootsie to the dog run. Once there, we had company: our friend Diane and her Boston terrier, Lucy, who chased a tennis ball the whole time. While Tootsie wandered around, Diane and I had good chats. She worked in one of the financial buildings nearby. We often visited each other's homes with the dogs in tow. When they came to our place, Lucy and Toots lay together on our living room sectional. Lucy was small enough to be Tootsie's baby, and it was fun to see them together.

My work day was long and busy, and I loved it. Living in New York with all its wonders was heaven. Chance meetings with Judy Collins, Tina Turner, Janet Jackson, and Madonna, in addition to Dick Van Dyke, David Cassidy, Barry Manilow, and many others were a common occurrence. One evening, Diane Keaton sat next to us at a movie. We were quiet and respected her privacy. I met great authors at readings, including Toni Morrison, Frank McCourt, Amy Tan, August Wilson, and Fran Lebowitz. It was a wonderful life, so full of interesting people, places, and things.

Often, we walked along the river, especially in the quiet of early morning. We had the best life, and we knew it. Sharing all of it with our pet made it even more special. One wonderful day as we walked toward the towers, we heard music and saw a small group of people gathered ahead, enjoying the lovely music. Pete Seeger, one of my many heroes in life, was giving an impromptu concert near his boat, *the Clearwater*. Though I had attended many of his concerts before, I will always remember this one as the best.

Chapter 4

A Day Like No Other

Since my work days were so long, I chose to get to the polling place at six in the morning, when it opened. I was the first one there and voted for Mark Green. It was a gorgeous fall day, crisp and sunny. I took a cab to get to work on time. My company, MTV Networks, was located in Times Square at 1515 Broadway.

My department, Media Services, was the source of press information for the company. At that time, online services were not available to us, so each day we read several national and local daily newspapers, weekly and monthly magazines, and newsletters for information on the entertainment industry. Before noon each day, there was a digest of our findings on the desks of every department in the company. In addition, our library kept extensive files with all of this information, which we provided upon request.

There were five of us to perform this service. I was always the first in, since I lived in the city. On this beautiful morning, I put the coffee on and began to scan the *New York Times*.

Suddenly, a loud clap of thunder shook the building. Thunder? How could it be? I stood at my window on the fifteenth floor overlooking Times Square and could see across the river to New Jersey. There wasn't a cloud anywhere in the deep blue and sunny sky.

I turned my TV to *Good Morning America*, whose studio was across the street from my building. A small plane had crashed into the World Trade Center, they announced. *OMG—our neighborhood!* The thunder I had heard was actually the sound of a crash almost four miles away. There was footage shown a few moments later.

My first thought was to call home, and my heart was filled with dread as I did. Our apartment was a few short blocks from the towers. No answer—Tom and Tootsie must be out for a walk. *OMG, are they OK?* I left a message and continued to watch the news for further details.

My staff members had begun to arrive, and they ran to my office to check the TV. They were breathless and frightened, having heard bits of news on the way from their trains from Brooklyn, Queens, and Long Island. *Had Tom and Tootsie been close to the crash?* The news now reported that the planes were not small at all but passenger planes out of major airports. I kept calling Tom. *Were he and Toots all right?*

Finally, he answered, in a state of shock. "It's terrible! The first tower is burning! I had Toots in the dog run and saw debris flying out of the top floors. It wasn't debris—it was people jumping from the burning building! It was a large plane that crashed into the building. What should I do? I sent Linda home."

Somehow, I kept myself calm listening to Tom. Finally, I told him, "Remember, the Museum of Jewish Heritage is right next door. That could be a target! Take some water and dog food. There are bags in the kitchen cabinet. I have some cash in my top dresser drawer. Take it all just in case! You and Tootsie can walk over to the East Side and then up to Fifty-Seventh Street. I'll call our friend Lizanne. She'll be happy to have you there, and I'll join you after work. Call me when you get there!"

As we spoke, I heard a loud, almost deafening, roar over the phone. It was the second plane, which would hit the second tower.

"The building is shaking!" Tom said.

"Hurry," I told him. "You and Tootsie get out! Call me when you can!"

I couldn't imagine what might happen next. How could this be happening? Was it safe to be anywhere in our city? (It was later reported that the second plane should have imploded prior to the tower's hit because of its tremendous speed.)

Soon we received a message from MTV Networks corporate headquarters that everyone should meet at noon in the cafeteria. We hurried to get our digest to the copy center for distribution. Everyone was worried about what might happen next, and it was hard to concentrate on business.

Once the meeting assembled, we were told to leave and to return to work only when it was declared safe and free of further danger. Donna, my staff member, was able to get a ride home with her husband, a police officer. I had planned to get to Lizanne's as soon as possible. Richard, our great librarian, reminded us all to visit the cash machine. As it turned out, he was right—the machines did go down along with cell phones and the transmitters for one of the major TV networks, which had been located inside the Twin Towers.

When I think back, I can't believe how calm and collected I remained. My heart pounds as I write this now, but my wits ruled when I needed them. As soon as two of my staff left, I straightened my desk and called our sons in LA to let them know that the three of us were OK.

My dearest friend for life, Sue, called and told me to get to her apartment on the upper West Side as soon as we could. Management would have the keys for us. "Stay as long as you need to! I wish I were there to help! This is awful!"

I assured her that we would get to her place after spending one night at Lizanne's apartment, where we had planned to meet.

Lisa, who worked with me, and Rose from the legal department joined me for the walk to Lizanne's. We were at Forty-Fourth Street and

Broadway; Lizanne was at Second Avenue and Fifty-Seventh Street. We walked straight across the city to Third Avenue, where we saw throngs of people filling the street and walking uptown together. There were no cars, no buses, no trucks, and few bicycles in sight. Now and then a police car appeared in a closed lane on its way somewhere. It was surreal!

New Yorkers are brisk walkers, and most were dressed in business attire and carrying briefcases or backpacks. A memorable and touching sight was that of two young black men carrying a frail old man wearing a yarmulke in their handmade "chair seat." People became neighbors, sharing information and advice—strangers no longer. Most were calm and helpful; some seemed in shock, unable to fathom what was happening or to think about what else was ahead. I was hopeful that Tom and Tootsie would get to Lizanne's very soon. We would stay there for one night and then go to the West Side.

Lisa, Rose, and I reached Fifty-Seventh Street and were welcomed by Lizanne. "Please use the telephone if you need it," she told us. "Lunch is ready." Music to our weary bones! One of her apartment windows afforded a view of the Third Avenue Bridge, which was filled with people from every walk of life, and of every color and size, walking to Brooklyn. All transportation was down.

After lunch, Rose and Lisa quickly found ways to get home. When they left, Lizanne and I discussed plans for the next few hours. After a glass of wine, we would find an open neighborhood restaurant for dinner. Hopefully, we would soon hear from Tom. I thought he and Tootsie would have been there by this time. What could have happened? Why hadn't he called? Where were they? It was so hard not to worry!

★ ★ ★

Finally, after Lizanne and I had dinner that night, Tom called. Following the second plane crash, he and Tootsie had gone to the lobby of our building, where there were police directing people to evacuate to New Jersey via the river. Vessels were waiting at the nearest landing.

Most of the residents had followed the directions of the police and proceeded to the riverfront. There were sailboats, Circle Line tour boats, tugboats, and yachts waiting to help in the evacuation. Steve, one of our neighbors, had his dog, Lila, a beautiful Rhodesian ridgeback, and suggested that he and Tom travel together with their dogs. They boarded a Moran tugboat; its job was usually to escort large ships and barges up and down the river.

Tootsie lay right down beside Tom. This experience was a first for her. Others aboard included a nun, a policeman who seemed to be ill, and many residents with their birds, cats, and dogs. Thoughts of Dunkirk and Noah's Ark crossed Tom's mind while the vessels headed for Secaucus, New Jersey.

As they arrived at their destination, a surreal image tested everyone's sense of reality. Across the river, to the horror of all aboard, one of the Trade Center towers collapsed.

Passengers and pets followed directions to an office building nearby, where water, telephones, and other necessities were provided. The company became a true port in a storm. What to do next? How long would this group of four have to remain in New Jersey?

Steve suggested they find a place to spend the night, just in case. As they walked along the street bordering the river, a doorman waved and asked if they wanted to buy an apartment. They declined but acknowledged their need for a place for themselves and their dogs to sleep that night. With the doorman's help, they rented a large corporate apartment: $100 just for the night, and Toots and Lila were included. Perfect!

Steve offered to shop while Tom watched the dogs. Lila had a reputation for getting around. She was able to turn doorknobs and push elevator buttons. Amazing! (In Africa, I'm told, ridgebacks help to hunt lions.) Toots had recovered from her first boat ride and, being a couch potato, would not be a worry. Tom's job was to keep Lila away from the door.

Steve was back soon with food for all, and they had a quiet and short evening. Both planned to get back to New York the next day.

★ ★ ★

Hearing from Tom calmed my fears. He and Tootsie were OK and would be back soon. After a good dinner on the next street over, Lizanne and I headed home. As we passed Third Avenue on the way back, we heard sounds of heavy traffic. Large trucks carrying all kinds of heavy equipment could be seen driving down Third Avenue for blocks, all headed to Ground Zero in Battery Park City. Volunteers had started to arrive from everywhere possible. And that was just the beginning of the help that would pour into our wounded city.

Encouraged and relieved by what we had seen, and back at Lizanne's, I had a wonderful night's sleep. After coffee in the morning, I headed to Bloomingdale's, my favorite store, which was conveniently on my way to work. I bought Tom and I two sets of clothes each to take with us to Sue's. We would spend tonight at Lizanne's and cross Manhattan the next morning.

While I was in the men's department, the front door opened and a woman called out, "The firemen need white socks. Please let me have as many white socks as you can. I'll take them to the firehouses." Moments later, she left with two large bags full of white socks. New York, New York—a wonderful town with wonderful people!

At my office, I would be alone most of that day. Only people who lived in the city could make it in to work. My phone was filled with messages from everywhere: friends, relatives, business people, all offering solace, suggesting ways to help, asking for details, and wishing us all well. I kept wondering whether we knew anyone killed in the towers. It was so terribly sad and tragic. By early afternoon, Tom called from Lizanne's and explained how he and Tootsie had returned from New Jersey.

"Well, Toots and I went for our early morning walk and to find transportation to the PATH train" (which tunnels under the Hudson to New York City's midtown). "I hailed several cabs, who all refused to take a dog."

"Why?" I asked him.

"Some people from countries in the Middle East are uncomfortable with dogs," he told me. Actually, he had told me that once before.

"Fortunately," he went on, "a couple came out of the building, asked if I needed help, and offered us a ride to the PATH train. They introduced themselves: she was secretary to Henry Kissinger, former secretary of state, and he was her husband from South America. They kindly drove us to the station, inquired whether or not trains were running, and made sure dogs were permitted. 'Yes and yes' were the answers. I thanked them for their kindness, and Toots and I walked to the platform.

"The train was crowded with people who had essential-service jobs across the river—restaurant workers, maintenance persons, etc. Again, Tootsie took all that was happening in stride. Through it all, she was wonderful. In a short time, we reached the West Side of the city, where there were several cabs. I waved a twenty-dollar bill and asked a driver to take us to the East Side and Fifty-Seventh. The driver had no problem with Tootsie, and here we are!"

"Oh, I'm so happy to hear that!" I said with a sigh of relief. "I'll be there soon."

Unfortunately, Tom forgot to walk Tootsie on the way to Lizanne's, and a lovely carpet in her living room had to be scrubbed. He soon found a park in the neighborhood.

Back at my office, I answered calls, put a digest together for the next day, and took myself and my new clothes back to Fifty-Seventh Street.

It was so wonderful to see Tom and Toots after what seemed like a very long time. After a quick walk in the park, they napped while Lizanne and I shopped for dinner makings—plus toothbrushes, etc.—to pack for our trip to the West Side in the morning.

★ ★ ★

Off we went soon after breakfast, with a borrowed laundry cart holding our belongings and Tootsie's food, water, and dishes. Lizanne had provided a haven for us, and we were very grateful. We headed straight across town to Sue's apartment near Lincoln Center.

On our way, we passed long lines of people outside a building. They were there to donate blood for victims of the tower crashes. Almost three thousand people had perished, and blood would not help them. But, of course, it would help others in need.

We began to think about people we knew who worked in or near the towers, including Ling Ling, Tom's Chinese teacher, who worked for *China Daily* in the second tower, and two neighbors from our apartment building, employees in the towers' lower level who had stands and shops along the way to the trains. We were so very grateful to be safe and well, so sad for those who were gone, and so thankful for all the kindnesses we and others received. Help from all over the country was already there or on the way.

We felt much like refugees in wars past and present, I think, walking with our cart and our dear Tootsie. As we approached Central Park, we decided to take a break and sat down on a bench. Tootsie found some soft grass and lay down.

"Can you spare some money for food for the homeless?" a pair of men asked.

Tom handed them some cash and said, "We're homeless too."

In fifteen minutes more, we arrived at Sue's apartment. The keys were with the doorman, and we were welcomed. We had no idea when we would be able to return to Battery Park. For the time being, this would be our home. Tootsie found a soft spot and took a nap while we got settled and made a list for the grocery store.

The sound of the pouring rain that night was muted by the roar of a jet fighter circling the city. Both sounds were somehow comforting, almost enveloping us and easing our anxieties. The king-size bed had room for the three of us. We slept peacefully, convinced that we were safe.

In the morning, Tom took Toots to the park, and I got ready for work. The subway was close by. Tom planned to call his clients to say that we were safe and together. Linda, his assistant, would come by to work with him as soon as transportation was available.

★ ★ ★

In a few days, many people were able to get back to work at my office. Everyone had a story to share and was worried about those who might have perished. A young woman who worked close to me had recently married a fireman. He was trapped with others in the first tower and died.

Weeks later, his funeral was held at St. Patrick's Cathedral. Many of us attended. Fifth Avenue was lined for miles with cars and trucks from fire company members who had traveled miles to support their fellow first responders. The church was filled with blue uniforms. It was so hard not to cry for our friend and for all the brave first responders who had given their lives for others.

★ ★ ★

Of course, there were very good restaurants in Sue's neighborhood. It was Lincoln Center. Our favorite, Fiorello's, had quite a few tables outside, and we were allowed to have Tootsie with us. The waiter brought a bone and a bowl of water for her, and she lay at our feet while we had a special dinner. A few other dogs were there, and all were well-behaved.

After two weeks, we were notified that we could return to Battery Park City. However, it still was not open to regular traffic. Linda came to help us pack up. I called Sue to thank her and let her know we'd leave the keys with the doorman. We were able to hail a cab, and the driver helped to pack the three of us with Tootsie and all our belongings into his car.

We rode as far as we could until barriers at the edge of Battery Park City prevented any unauthorized vehicle from going farther. We still had more than a few blocks to get to our building. The air was gray and thick with dust as we walked right by Ground Zero. Tents were set up where workers could rest, get treatment, or have a massage. Boats, large and small, stood by. One served as a cafeteria, where volunteers fed shift after shift of workers who had come to help. There were greyhounds and other dogs brought in to help with therapy. People wanted to help in every way possible.

As we passed a worker sitting on a bridge support, I thanked him for coming to help. "I wouldn't be anywhere else," he replied. As we walked on, we smiled and thanked all those we could. Some petted Tootsie. Others, busy at their tasks, just nodded.

Soon, we reached our home, where the air was not as dark and thick as what we'd encountered almost a mile away. We stopped at the dog run first. Tootsie began to smile a lot. Home at last!

It was great to see our doorman and the staff. They had done a great job of caring for the building and our apartments. We were told that looters had tried to break in and were stopped. The stores in the neighborhood had not fared as well. They were emptied out totally.

What a welcome sight—our own apartment! "Thank goodness you closed the windows before you left, Tom," I noted. "There would have been dust everywhere. Instead, the place is almost as clean as you left it that day. Thank you for remembering to do that."

The fridge and freezer were empty of spoiled food. The staff had done a great job. Life would be quite different now, but we were home in a beautiful area close to friends and favorite restaurants, and we would be sleeping in our own soft beds.

Much to do: groceries, laundry ... One restaurant was open and permitted pets to lie under the tables. Tootsie was happy, and we felt as though we were dining in Paris, where dogs are allowed to lie under tables. We tried to imagine what it had been like to have been a refugee in Europe during WWII, returning to our village that had been attacked. Actually, in a way, we were refugees. Many of our neighbors had not yet returned. Some would not return at all.

Of course, the subway station in the towers was gone, so I would have to walk several blocks east to get a train to work. There were National Guard members on each block. Until they knew us, we were asked for ID each day. They were camped in Battery Park itself. One night I baked and wrapped dozens of snickerdoodles and delivered them the next morning to the guard at the entrance of the camp. I hope the cookies helped to make them feel welcome and appreciated.

For weeks afterward, groups of volunteers appeared from everywhere, it seemed. Many were religious groups. They cleaned apartments and offered help of all kinds to the residents. Tom and Tootsie met a group while taking a walk one afternoon. They asked Tom to join them in prayer. I wish I had a photo of that moment. It would remind me of the kind and caring people who came to help those of us affected by the attack, and Tootsie would have been in the picture too, probably standing quietly by. (Greyhounds are not comfortable sitting. Their conformation causes them to prefer lying down to rest to sitting on their hindquarters.)

One morning, I heard activity outside the kitchen window. EPA workers in hazmat suits were emptying the children's sandbox. Once young children had enjoyed this place; now it was a hazard and had to be removed. All over the city, one could feel the warmth and compassion brought to us from all over our country. How long would the care and kindness remain? How many times do we need to be reminded that "we belong to each other"[2]?

---

[2] Part of a quote attributed to Mother Teresa.

Chapter 5

The Order of Life: Change

After 9/11, my workplace seemed different. Life in the city was certainly different. Our car was buried under rubble in the building next door. Stores and shops opened slowly—except for the ones in the towers, of course. Each day, the *New York Times* published a list of those who perished in and near the towers, with touching stories about friends, neighbors, coworkers, first responders ... all who mattered in all our lives. On 9/11, 2,996 souls were lost, including the nineteen terrorists. People from seventy-eight countries died that day in New York, Pennsylvania, and Washington, DC. We had to be so grateful that we were safe and back in our home.

In a few weeks, we learned that my company had planned a massive restructuring in the month of September. Of course, it was postponed for a short time due to 9/11. Every department was affected, mine almost totally. Richard, a wonderful person I had recently hired, would remain. Lisa, Donna, and I were to leave.

My boss and I had worked together for over fifteen years, and it was hard for us both to handle what was happening. Although I was past retirement age, it was a blow, and the timing was harsh. But everyone was treated fairly and properly. I had loved my job working with young and creative people in the entertainment industry. I loved New York and its energy. It had been almost twenty years! It was hard to hold back the tears. What to do next?

★ ★ ★

It was good to get home that night, where a hug and smiles and a wagging tail were my greeting.

"How was your day, dear?" Tom asked.

"Not so great, thanks. Let's have dinner and we'll talk."

And so we did. I had been totally surprised by the company's restructuring. After the shock of 9/11, I felt very vulnerable and uncertain about the future.

Tom listened carefully, then said, "I can work anywhere. We don't have to stay in New York. Why don't we move back to Lakeridge in Connecticut?"

"Of course!" I said. "I can't think of a better place to be, and Tootsie will love it! We'll call Nate and Shirley in the real estate office and see what they have available. We can go up this weekend."

The next day at work, I bargained for an additional year of work, which would make my years at MTV Networks number an even twenty. My request was granted and allowed me enough time to leave my department in the best order. That meant a great deal to me.

The future home we found in Connecticut gave us a challenge. Along with a few repairs, we had furniture to remove and decorating to do. We drove up most weekends for the following year. Lizanne came along to help, and Bruce and Wing Kee shared great ideas for color and design when they visited. They even helped with furniture shopping.

Tom was still recovering from all he had witnessed in New York. An organization (World Trade Center Health Program) had been set up to assist survivors of 9/11. People there were very helpful and continue to be available to all who need them. Keeping busy was always my therapy. Still, I have moments of sadness along with anxiety dreams. Few can forget that tragic time in our history.

Spending more time with Tootsie was wonderful for both of us. We took her almost everywhere, and when we couldn't, we had Cathy, a great friend and community employee, care for her. We were able to visit Eileen often on our drive up to the country, and sometimes on the way back. One day, Petco had a great sale on stuffed dog toys, and we took a bunch of them to her hounds, who had a wild party with them.

Each year, Eileen had a fundraiser to help meet her costs. People brought their hounds and enjoyed games, food, items for sale, a raffle, etc. Her many friends and supporters helped in every way possible. We always attended with Tootsie, who loved the burgers best.

Our final year in Manhattan passed quickly. The thought of moving was almost overwhelming: too many clothes, too much furniture, too much of everything! Thank goodness for the moving company and the Salvation Army. On the last day, Tom took Toots and a few items up to Connecticut, while I made certain the apartment was cleared out and clean. I would miss the doormen and other employees along with our neighbors—and, of course, our doctors, and Tootsie's vet. Everything about our almost thirty years in New York City would be etched in our minds forever. We knew it would survive without us and recover from 9/11, just as we would.

Decorating, arranging, and settling in to our new place kept me busy, and Toots was always available to hug and pet or walk. Tom worked in his office upstairs, and in our down time we could go for a swim across the street or get a game of tennis in. There was a very good veterinary hospital in the next town. They began to offer training classes for dogs, and Tootsie and I signed up. She had only had basic training on the track, and we had not taught her all the commands available and useful for safety in our new environment, where there were more animals to encounter—both tame and wild.

Six other dogs and their owners joined us for the classes. The teacher was great, and I was hopeful. It was hard work for dogs and owners alike. On the second day, we were asked to walk a short way with our dogs and then to tell them to "Stay." We were to walk on alone—which I would do, hopeful that Toots would obey. Each time I thought I was succeeding, I would hear a burst of laughter and turn around to see Tootsie right behind me—very embarrassing! The other dogs had obeyed.

Eventually, we failed the class. However, I was determined, and Toots and I did private lessons in early mornings at home and had success, thank goodness. It cost me many bags of treats.

★ ★ ★

Early in October of that year, we planned a drive to Florida, with a stop on the way at my alma mater, Mary Washington College, in Fredericksburg, Virginia. Tootsie would stay with Eileen, where she would have greyhound friends with whom to play. Eileen had been keeping her eye out for a companion for Toots. "I might have a good fit for Tootsie. Her name is Judge Judy, and I'll see how they get along together and let you know when you return."

It was great to visit my school and recall a life-changing four years as a "stranger in a strange land."[3] Next, we would stop in North Carolina.

In Florida, we stayed in an oceanfront house in Boynton Beach for a wonderful week. Walking on a peaceful, sandy shore early in the morning, visiting a drive-through zoo where giraffes would block our roadway and bend down to look through our windows, and visiting the Morikami Museum and Japanese Gardens in del Rey—all these experiences combined to make a great vacation.

---

[3] Exodus 2:22: Following the birth of his son, Moses compared his time in Egypt with being "a stranger in a strange land." Also the title of a book by Robert A. Heinlein and a song by Leon Russell.

There was a pet store with dogs for sale nearby. A miniature greyhound was in a "crib" near the entrance. We stopped each day to visit. We really missed Tootsie! Good food and the change of pace made us feel renewed before the trip home.

When we got to Virginia, we stayed the night. Early the next morning, the TV news was focused on Torrington, Connecticut—our town. The mayor was speaking. A snow and ice storm had hit New England, and many areas were without electricity and basic services.

We called Eileen, who was OK—and Tootsie and the other hounds were too. We called Tom's sister, Betty, in Norwalk to see if we could stop to stay with her until it was safe to pick up Tootsie and get home. She said that would be fine.

We called our community. Thank goodness, the maintenance department was hard at work and expected we would have heat and light in a day or so. We had a nice visit and dinner with Betty and then called Eileen to say that we could be there the next afternoon. She told us that Tootsie had made a friend—another black hound about her age, named Billie. Judge Judy and Tootsie had not bonded. The Judge was not very social, and Eileen recalled that when she took Judge Judy from the track, the workers had said, "Thank goodness you're taking her out of here!" They didn't give a reason.

Billie had been with a family for a short time but had trouble being patient with small children. The family had reluctantly returned her not long ago. "See what you think," said Eileen. "She might be a good companion for Toots." I hoped that Billie might be the answer to Tootsie's separation anxiety.

Chapter 6
Celia

Celia, twin sister

AND, I WAS RIGHT. TOOTSIE AND BILLIE SEEMED TO HAVE KNOWN each other in another life, and both happily jumped into our car for the ride to Torrington. There were a few growls while they adjusted to the available space, and then a quiet trip. A quick stop at Petco for supplies, and we were there in two hours.

The house had been warming up slowly, but it was chilly still. After a brisk walk, we showed Billie her new home. While I began to make dinner, Tom opened the pantry door to get dog food. There was a large bag of it, I remembered.

"OMG! There's a family of mice living in the bag of food!" Tom yelled.

And so there was. It had been a really cold winter, and mice were apt to invade any warm buildings available. When food was also there for the taking, they really moved in! (Once, years before, I had left an open box of spaghetti in a drawer for the winter. No surprise—in the spring, I found that mice had moved in). The bag and the family went out to the trash with Tom, who then returned to Petco for another supply.

Having had two brothers and then two baby boys, I felt the need for some females in the house, and I had many favorite girly names ready for our hounds. We loved the song "Cecelia" by Paul Simon, along with almost every song he ever wrote and sang with Art Garfunkel, and decided to rename Billie to Celia. I emailed the former owners to say how happy we were to have Celia and explained the name change. They had named her Billie in honor of Billie Holiday, a wonderful blues singer from the past. They were happy to hear that she had a new home. They had kept a photo of her in a place of honor in their home—very nice people!

Celia had sad brown eyes and only bits of white markings on her paws. She had come from a family home and knew how to live in a house. She and Tootsie followed us and each other wherever we went and seemed to love each other. There were enough soft places for each to be comfortable. Neither seemed territorial, and when they could, they shared soft spaces. They had separate beds in our bedroom at night, and they slept soundly even when owls were hooting in the trees outside.

We had been told that Celia often had nightmares. Sometimes Toots did also. Sometimes their legs moved in their sleep as though they were racing. Memories of the track, I assumed. One night, a sudden sharp clap of thunder preceded a heavy rainstorm. In a flash, we had two black hounds between us in our bed, which thankfully was king-size!

Our house was located up a hill and across from one of the recreation lodges. Often, deer were playing or sleeping in the woods outside. It was not unusual to see a pileated woodpecker at work on a tree. I watched a fawn taking a peaceful nap under a tree one day and wished I had a camera with a long-distance lens.

We had to be careful when we walked two black dogs at night. Flashlights were always in hand, and we watched carefully for traffic. Often we went into the lodge parking lot, which was next to tennis courts surrounded by tall trees.

As we walked one night, I heard the snapping of branches on my left. When I looked up, I saw a light-colored animal on a thick branch of the tree. I held in my feeling of terror and took a deep breath.

"Tom," I said calmly, "start walking back across the street and up to the house. Speak softly and don't run. I'll tell you why when we get inside."

Once inside he was amazed to hear what I was sure I saw. It was a big cat!

My suspicion was confirmed the next day by our night security guard. "Yes," he told us, "the state of Connecticut doesn't acknowledge that we have mountain lions here—if they did so, they would have to conserve them—but these cats have been seen in a few places near us lately. They are not aggressive unless provoked. They move from place to place quietly, usually staying about a month in each. You did the right thing by walking away quietly."

Weeks later, there was a photo of a similar cat spotted a few towns away. *Whew!* Walking at night after that, we were wary and spoke loudly so that any creatures would be sure to hear us coming.

★ ★ ★

Some of our city friends worried that our large dogs could spot a rabbit and pull us down and through the woods or to the lake. We didn't worry; they were well-behaved. When I had short errands to do, I took the girls along for the ride unless the weather was very hot. They seemed to enjoy it.

As we returned one day and I opened the back of the car and leashed them up, a friend appeared across the street. She was walking her sister's little dog. Celia spotted the dog and freaked out, making a lunge to head across the street.

Both hounds had stretchable leashes. The next thing I knew, I was wrapped like a mummy and falling backward to the pavement. My arms were tied to my sides. No part of my body could bend except my neck.

OMG, I thought. *My head will hit the pavement and I will be unconscious. I might die!* I heard my head as it hit the pavement and bounced. I was still conscious, and I was still alive, and I was very surprised.

Meanwhile, my friend tied her little dog to a tree and came to my aid. After she unwound the leashes, she waited while I pulled myself together enough to sit up and let her know I was OK. I couldn't believe it, but just fifteen minutes later, we walked up the hill to my house with the dogs in tow. I assured Marilyn that I would be all right. I had an ice pack, and I would relax in a chair with my feet on a hassock. Tom was downtown, so I had time to recuperate. The girls lay end to end on the couch nearby.

When he got home, Tom was horrified to hear what had happened. Marilyn called later to make sure I was OK. I was. The next day, I went to our doctor. He declared that I was fine. *How hard can a head be?* I wondered.

Not long after that, we walked the girls to the stable to help decorate for a Halloween Ghost Walk. We tied their leashes to a tent pole so that we had hands free. Suddenly, the tent collapsed, the leashes snapped, and we watched Toots and Celia head for the woods to chase a rabbit they saw. Fortunately, the rabbit escaped. The girls had stopped at the edge of the thick woods—unfamiliar territory for them.

It was another close call, and no wonder! Greyhounds are trained at the tracks to chase a rabbit—not a real one, thank goodness, but a replica—as a lure. Though we lived in a forest, we had seen no rabbits in our area. But the stable area with the gardens nearby surely attracted all manner of wildlife looking for food. (There was not a rabbit included in our collection of stuffed animal toys.)

We loved our new house and everything about it, except the long hill of steps from our parking space to our front door. Thank goodness for grocery carts and strong arms! But even they were not a lot of help when snow covered the ground. We were growing older and began to think of the future. We'd been there for a few years. We needed a garage and a flat place to live, we decided.

Here we go again, I thought.

We began to look and found a larger (and flatter) place. The house had three floors and an attic. The deck was spacious and on the edge of the woods. We put our "hill" house on the market and bought the new one.

In the meantime, we had planned a trip to Europe even before we left New York. Eileen agreed to take Tootsie and Celia, who would be happy to be with their greyhound friends for a while.

★ ★ ★

The river cruise was great fun. Wing Kee and Bruce, our designer friends, were with us, along with a few others we knew. The trip was down the Rhine River from Brussels to Switzerland, with stops in Germany, France, Holland, and Switzerland. It was fabulous, historic, and memorable. In the middle of it, we had a phone call from our realtors telling us that our house had sold. Great news, and cause for celebration—and another move.

Our trip had been that of a lifetime, and now we planned to enjoy our community by becoming more involved in activities with friends and neighbors. The girls loved the new house and spent time on all three floors each day. Sometimes they just followed the sun, but mostly they followed us. Sometimes they carried their toys along with them. Their favorites were teddy bears.

In the summer, the deck was their choice. There they could watch people walking by while lying on soft mats in the fresh air. Best of all, we could walk to the stable each day to enjoy the dog run and greet all the animals. Toots and Celia were great pals with each other and us. Of the two, Tootsie was the most fun outside.

One day, I leashed them up for a stable walk. Halfway up the trail, I realized that Tootsie, who was in the lead, was not attached to her leash.

"Tootsie, come get a cookie! Tootsie …" No matter what I said to her, she kept on walking. *What if she sees a rabbit? She'll be off like a shot! OMG!* Heaven knows how long it would take to find her. Hounds, not just greyhounds, are known to go far once they begin to run loose. They love it! *How far would she go? What if she gets caught in some brambles or hurts herself?* Thank goodness she was not in an open area.

Soon, as luck would have it, she stopped to sniff a plant. Whew! Tootsie was a smart cookie and gave me a smile as I snapped the leash to her collar. What a trickster!

Somewhat surprisingly, Celia slowly became more of an alpha dog, taking the lead when we walked, being first in line for a treat. Tootsie took it all in stride and didn't compete with her sister.

When our sons John and Tom came to visit, they loved taking the sisters for long walks, even in winter. We got more than our share of snow, and it was beautiful, especially to the California boys. The girls preferred the dog run in winter because the soft snow covered the pebbles used to line the run, which hurt their paws. The boys and the girls didn't seem to mind the cold at all.

★ ★ ★

Sometimes when we put on her fleecy winter coat, Celia would cry in pain. A trip to Canton and our vet didn't get to the cause, though we had several tests done. To avoid problems, I made sure that everyone was aware of Celia's sensitivity. Whenever I sat on a sofa, she would cuddle close and stare at me with soulful eyes until I began to pet her (softly, of course). We had many of these special times together.

Celia had minor health issues now and then. Several times, I took her to the vet while Toots stayed at home with Tom. One day, when our sons took the girls to the dog run, Celia had a wheezing episode and they rushed her to Canton, where she received an allergy shot and then was fine. Fortunately, we had pet health insurance. Celia still had her sensitive spot, and still there was no diagnosis. We made sure to remind visitors to be careful about petting her.

Between volunteer work and care of the dogs, we were busy enough in retirement. Life went along happily until one day, as I walked Celia (while Tom walked Tootsie), she fell onto her side and couldn't get up. Something serious was happening.

Tom and Toots stood by while I got the car. We lay Celia in the back, and I drove straight to our vet. My disc player was on, and Simon and Garfunkel were singing "Cecilia." It brought tears to my eyes.

On arrival, I called for help getting Celia out of the car. They took her right into an examining room. It was late in the afternoon, and the office was not equipped to keep her overnight. They suggested that I take her to the next town, where there was evening emergency care and they could keep her until morning. It was half an hour away.

When we arrived, the staff there came out to get her. She cried while they moved her inside. I was asked to pick her up before eight o'clock the next morning when our Canton vet would be open.

Driving home was difficult, knowing how sick Celia seemed to be. What could have happened to her? It was sad to have an evening without her. We had a quiet dinner and retired early so I could get up to bring Celia back to Canton where I hoped they could make her better. A restless night ensued.

It was a beautiful spring morning as I drove through our countryside heading for the overnight veterinary hospital. When I arrived, I was anxious to know Celia's condition. She had had a quiet night, I was told. Two kind assistants carried her out to the car. "Good girl, Celia! We'll get you better in a little while."

But when we arrived in Canton and helpers tried to take her out of the car, she screamed and growled and had to be muzzled. The doctor promised to examine her further and call me when he finished. My heart was not filled with hope. I tried to keep busy and not think the worst.

When the call came, we knew what had to be done and asked a kind neighbor to sit with Tootsie while we said goodbye to Celia. Tom hadn't been with me when Ping Ping went to sleep, so this experience would be new for him. Understandably, people find it difficult to witness such a sad moment. It is difficult, but not staying would be more difficult for me as our dear pet left our world. We brought her into our family, and we owed her a kind departure.

Celia seemed not even to recognize us when we entered the quiet room where she lay still on a blanket watching us. We spoke softly and petted her gently. "We love you, Celia. You've been a good girl, and a good sister to Tootsie!" We hoped that our touches told her how hard it was for us to let her go and how much we loved her and how much she would be missed.

Dr. Evans gave us a few more minutes to say goodbye and then made the heartbreaking process go as smoothly as possible. It was a peaceful passing and terribly sad. Celia was almost twelve years old, a pretty good age considering her history. The lifespan of a greyhound generally runs for ten to fifteen years. It was April 20, 2004.

Celia, you truly broke our hearts. We miss you still.

Chapter 7

Tootsie and Miss Daisy

sweet friends

RETURNING HOME FROM OUR SAD AFTERNOON WITH CELIA, WE found a basket of flowers lying at our front door. Tom's sister had sent them. We had picked Tootsie up from our neighbor's house on our way back from Canton. I decided to place the flowers on the deck in the shade. A few minutes later, there was Tootsie, lying down next to the basket. She seemed to sense what had happened and why the flowers were there.

I wrote to Celia's former family, and they answered with kind condolences. A week or so later, it was time to ask Eileen about another hound. Tootsie was very lonely, and so were we.

Jeanne Cassidy

"Oh, I'm sorry about Celia! What happened?" We hadn't taken time to call Eileen before this day. She agreed that we had done the right thing. "Oh," she said, "my friend in Litchfield just had his greyhound sent back to him. He's looking for someone to adopt her since his wife is ill and he's going to put his farm up for sale very soon. You can call him and go over there to meet Dixie and see if Tootsie and she could be friends."

And so we did.

★ ★ ★

Moo! Moo! Moo! A herd of black and white cows grazed in the field behind the barn. Mr. Moore watched from the porch of his old and historic farmhouse in Bethlehem, Connecticut, as his son, John led us to the old red barn. It was still standing after many years, empty except for supplies but still fragrant with the smell of animals—and a temporary home for a very shy hound named Showoff's Dixie who had finished her racing days.

John had to coax and lead her outside so that Tootsie and I could approach her. She was a reddish brindle and very timid. I spoke softly and held out my hand for her to sniff. Soon we were able to leash her, and she walked quite easily alongside Tootsie.

Tom and I agreed that the hounds seemed fine with each other, and we told Mr. Fitz we would like to adopt Dixie and that we would call Eileen to let her know. Time would tell what the future would bring, but today, it seemed it would be very bright.

"Tootsie! You'll have a new sister very soon!" We had to choose a more suitable name for this petite and ladylike hound, and it needed to sound similar to Dixie so that she could relate to it. Tom thought Daisy might be good, and I loved it! Sold!

A week later, we drove to Bethany. Eileen was ready for us. "She's out in the new shed and waiting for you all. Just sign the papers." While

Tom did the signing, Toots and I walked to the shed. "Come on, Toots. Let's take your new sister home." And there was Daisy, quietly waiting for us in the shed. It was so exciting to see her!

I attached the leash I had brought to her collar and we opened the door to leave. OMG! The leash had not attached as I thought! Daisy raced out of the door across the lawn, grabbed one of Eileen's geese by the neck, and headed for the main road. OMG! None of us could run forty miles an hour (the top greyhound speed). It wasn't a busy road, but …

Screech! The next-door neighbor happened to be returning home in his truck. He stopped short and jumped out and caught Daisy by the collar, causing her to drop the goose, who ran back to its gaggle as though nothing had happened. Well, so much for *shyness*. Thank goodness for neighbors! What had I been thinking? Had I forgotten that Daisy was first and foremost a hound? Big mistake!

★ ★ ★

Tootsie taught Daisy by example, and Daisy paid close attention. In no time, she became used to the routines and began to smile a lot. She and Toots became fast friends and often slept end-to-end on the couch.

It was a delight to see Daisy overcome her shyness and become Tootsie's shadow. Her big brown eyes followed whoever was in the room. People-watching was one of her favorite pastimes. She loved her walks, sun-bathing on the deck, and riding in the car. Her favorite toy was a stuffed gorilla. She seemed to enjoy it most when she lay on the couch with her head on its shoulder.

Off and on through my years, I had studied piano. Now that I was retired, I had time most days to play for my own enjoyment. Had I practiced more often, I might have been confident playing for others. However, I was very content with my audience of two, who always came into the room to listen. When I began to play, Toots and Daisy climbed onto the couch behind me and were the best audience I could ask for.

★ ★ ★

"Jeanne—Pull over! As fast as you can. Look up!"

Tom and I were on a two-lane road, heading to the next town to do some errands, with Toots and Daisy lying on the back seat. Suddenly, seemingly out of nowhere, a black car appeared, speeding toward us in *our* lane! The opposite lane was unusually busy with cars, bumper to bumper, driving back from our destination. Would we be hit? The lane was so narrow! I was a good driver, but where could I go? Could I get over the curb on my right in time? There was nowhere else to go!

In less than a minute, it was all over. The black car had sped by, missing us by inches, and there were four cars pulled over behind us! OMG! Toots and Daisy had been thrown out of the back seat into the trunk area, where they lay in a heap.

Tom opened his door. I exhaled a very long breath. None of the cars behind us had gotten a license number, Tom reported.

I checked the girls. "Daisy's foot is bleeding! Let's get to the vet's office!" Looking back, I saw that the other cars were letting us leave first. Perhaps it was taking them longer to get over the shocking near miss—not that we were totally over it. It was hard to believe that none of us was hit.

The animal-hospital parking lot was quite full, and that meant that lots of patients were waiting. We found seats and petted Toots and Daisy until they lay down next to us. There were birds, cats, one rabbit, and large and small canines waiting.

It was after three o'clock when the waiting room door opened and a man with a dog in his arms came in. *OMG, ooh, oh!* and other sounds of concern filled the room. The man responded, "It's not the first time. He never learns." One of the doctors came out and ushered the man and his dog—snout covered with quills—into a treatment room. A not-to-be-forgotten sight!

Thank goodness there were three doctors available that afternoon. Soon Daisy's foot was treated and bandaged, and we were on our way to our errands—and driving with extra care. Daisy's foot soon healed, and our lives went on. We hoped that the dog with the quills was OK and would finally learn a lesson.

★ ★ ★

At the time, I was working on marketing for our Lakeridge community and on the board of directors. I met a wonderful woman who had moved east from California and opened a photography studio nearby. She brought her young son along when she came to work with us. It was winter, and we'd had lots of snow, so we made time for sledding, walking, and skating. Kristen managed to take beautiful photos of our facilities along the way, and her shots of the outdoors were exquisite. When we stopped at our house for lunch, Toots and Daisy caught her creative eye, and the results were the beautiful shots of the two that you see in their chapters.

Soon, another winter melted into spring. It was time for filling the planters with geraniums and setting up the hammock; time for longer walks and soft mats out on the deck.

★ ★ ★

"Tom, Tom, wake up! The house alarm is going off! Get up quickly and throw some clothes on!"

We usually slept with the bedroom door open, but the night before, a fly had invaded and was driving us all crazy. We finally shooed him out the doorway and closed the bedroom door.

I jumped out of bed to open the door. The hallway was filled with a gray haze of smoke. The fire alarm was blaring! I grabbed my jeans, a shirt, and shoes. "Tom, get dressed and get the dogs leashed! We have to get out of here!"

Toots and Daisy jumped out of bed with Tom. The phone was ringing as I threw on my clothes, grabbed my purse, and hurried down the stairs. The kitchen was filled with smoke! And, of course, the phone stopped ringing as I got to it, but I called the security gate. The gate had monitored the alarm and called the fire department, which was on its way. In just a few minutes, the four of us were out in the street. It was eight o'clock on a Friday morning.

Our home was attached to two others. The firemen knocked at their doors and had the neighbors leave their homes just in case the fire spread. The people next door came out with a large briefcase filled with their important legal papers. I had not thought to do the same. Very important lesson!

Within a few minutes, the source of the fire was found to be the microwave oven in our kitchen. The smoke from the oven had permeated the entire house. The chief gave us a report and told us that one of us could go in to retrieve what we would need from the house, but we would not be able to stay there for any length of time. (Be they in New York, Litchfield, or almost anywhere in our country, firefighters are very special people—fearlessly risking their own lives to save the lives and property of others. From the World Trade Center to our house to "everywhere USA," their heroism is legend.)

Our neighbors kindly invited us for breakfast—dogs too. We sat on their deck and made plans for the near future. Where to stay? The house would be uninhabitable for quite a while.

Our friend Evelyn would not be up this weekend. We called, and she offered her home until we could find a rental. We called our realtors, who would show us a couple of homes the next day. The management office informed us that the insurance adjuster would be there that afternoon. Fueled with a wonderful breakfast and thanking our kind neighbors, we packed necessaries and drove to Evelyn's house.

Toots and Daisy had been there before and knew where the softest places were. After getting them settled, we shopped for whatever we needed. Later in the day, we looked at a few rentals and chose a well-worn but comfortable house within an easy walk of ours. It was on a cul-de-sac that lacked sufficient parking spaces, but we never minded an extra walk. The neighbors were friendly and welcoming. We could keep track of the cleaning and repairing going on at our house and easily walk to the dog run and stable after that.

The fire presented an opportunity to upgrade our kitchen and flooring. In a month, all was finished, and we moved back in. We learned that the microwave had self-imploded. The insurance adjuster told us there had been quite a few similar oven incidents nationwide in the past few years. We learned that despite the existence of many different name brands, only a few companies in Asia manufactured most of them. Life is so full of lessons to learn!

No matter where we were living, Toots and Daisy were happy. Being together was the most important thing to the four of us. We kept in close touch with Eileen. Often, she drove up to see us—once for Christmas. More often, we would go to Bethany and eat at her favorite diner, catching up on all the greyhound news.

Not long after that, Tom sold his business and was able to enjoy more of life in general. Tootsie and Daisy benefited from extra walks and many more hugs and pets.

In the meantime, Daisy experienced a strange accident. I had added two coverlets to the twin beds in our guestroom. They were cotton and made in India, and were meant to be decorative only. Often, the girls lay on the twin beds for a change of scene.

One morning, Daisy came down the stairs very slowly. We knew why when we noticed that her paws were bleeding under her toenails.

We called Canton and raced there to get their help. Who would have thought that the cause would be the coverlets! The fabric and the dyes used were abrasive and caused the injury and infection. She lost all her nails and had her paws bandaged for a few weeks. Thankfully, the nails grew back. So much for my accessorizing! (Some fabrics are troublesome for soft paws, and sometimes the dyes used in the fabric can be toxic for pets and humans as well.)

★ ★ ★

Litchfield, Torrington, and the surrounding area was home to many talented artists. During the month of August 2005, a charming nearby town, New Hartford, announced a fundraising event—Dog Daze of New Hartford—to support four local charities. For the auction, forty-five plaster casts of breeds of large dogs were sculpted and painted by artists who proposed designs to sponsors, who in turn made their choices. Following a parade of the dogs, they were placed all around New Hartford to be seen and to publicize the final event: the auction.

The auction was held in early October. There were four greyhounds among the plaster casts. The one I wanted most wore a flowered hat with a bee on top of it. I was bidding against a very determined man until I discovered that he was the husband of the artist who designed the dog. It was getting expensive, so I stopped. Tom and I won two of the three remaining. We attached *Salvadog Dali* and *Anubis* to a dolly to get them home safely.

When Tootsie and Daisy met us at the door, they stopped short and stared at what was coming in. Very slowly, they walked closer and then sniffed these unusual hounds repeatedly. It was a very funny moment! The shapes were right, but "the nose knows." (We still have Salvadog, who was decorated with Dali-like images. We gave Anubis, who was inspired by the ancient Egyptian god who ushered souls into the afterlife, to Eileen.)

At Christmas, John came from Los Angeles and decorated our tree. He spent many hours taking the girls for long walks in the snow-covered winter wonderland. Dogs and John knew how to dress for the weather, and we all enjoyed having John with us. We missed our sons, whose careers had taken them to the West Coast. Though we spoke on the phone almost every day, nothing takes the place of hugs and meals together, and so much else in life!

★ ★ ★

The dog run had many more visitors after our pet committee raised funds to make an agility course at its center. Our maintenance staff built a series of ramps and obstacle challenges to professional standards. What fun! We spent many hours encouraging Toots and Daisy to complete the course. Daisy was enthusiastic; Tootsie, not so much. Still, it was fun to keep trying.

Spring made a very short stop each year in Connecticut. First came the crocus breaking through the crust of snow. Following the snow melt, the pussy willows and daffodils appeared; then, at last, the tulips surfaced. Songs of birds, longer days, and warmer sun assured us that winter was over. Brooks and streams added their rippling sounds to the symphony of spring—a wonder of life on our earth.

Tootsie had lived a healthy life with us and each of her two sisters. She was almost thirteen and seemed to be slowing down. She fell one day but responded well to a massage and a checkup. It was hard to imagine life without her. But, as time went on, her energy level dwindled along with her appetite. Following a checkup during the summer, we realized that she might be suffering, and suffering was not an option we would choose. Too often, animals live for their companions, who wait too long to let them go.

We spent wonderful last days together before we scheduled a time for Tootsie to go to sleep. The night before we were to see Dr. Evans,

Tootsie fell off the couch and could hardly move. We called Canton, and they said they would stay open for us. It was six o'clock at night. Poor Daisy! We couldn't leave her alone, and we couldn't take her with us. I called our friend June, who agreed to come over and stay with Daisy.

"It's OK, Tootsie! You'll be all right soon. We love you, good girl!" As I leaned over the back seat, she moved away from me, so I stopped touching and just spoke softly. When we arrived at the hospital, Dr. Evans and an assistant came out to carry her in. In just a few minutes, she was gone. She would have died at home had we not called when we did.

Toot, Toot, Tootsie, goodbye! Beautiful Tootsie, you made us all cry! Thank you for all the joyful days and nights, all the laughs and smiles you brought to our lives!

Chapter 8

Miss Daisy

A dear girl

June and Daisy met us at the door after our sad and tearful ride home. We sat quietly for a while and hugged Daisy. June told us, "A while after you left, Daisy got up onto the couch with me and we watched television. Then, suddenly, she jumped down to the floor and stood still for a while, her ears perked. Then she climbed back on the couch. She seemed to sense what had happened."

June was right. *After all*, I thought, *Toots and Daisy were soul sisters.*

We had a trip to California planned and decided to board Daisy in Canton and not at Eileen's. I don't remember the reason. We made sure to send her special food and favorite mat and her gorilla with her.

Son John was making a film, and Tom's sister was going to Los Angeles with us. She loved movies and had wished to be an actress. It was our pleasure to share this opportunity with her. We did studio tours and had a wonderful trip.

Daisy did not fare as well. We had sent her with eight days of her food. She had barely eaten and had lost weight. Perhaps she would have been happier with Eileen and her hounds. It took a few weeks for her to get back most of her weight.

★ ★ ★

We rarely left Daisy alone. We knew that we could get through the winter, but we had to find another sister for her soon after that. It was only October and still not too cold.

Just before Halloween, the three of us took a morning trip to Canton. Talbot's was having a great sale! Plus, we needed a few groceries too. On the way back, it began to get very cold and to snow. By the time we reached the bottom of the hill up to our community, roads had gotten very slippery. There was a parking area halfway up, and we were barely able to get there. Several cars had pulled in before us.

As the snow grew heavier, people left their cars and began to walk the rest of the way. We followed, laden with packages and leading Daisy through the storm. When we got to our gate, we were very cold and stood packed inside the booth to warm up for a while.

Our wonderful friend Cathy came along in her truck and got us home. The forecast was grim. The staff was planning to spend the night due to terrible driving conditions, so I made several large pans of macaroni and cheese. Warm food would help us all. We went to bed early but were awakened in the middle of the night feeling very cold. We had lost electricity—no lights, no heat!

The next several days were a nightmare. This storm had paralyzed the Northeast. Cathy had managed to find doughnuts and to make coffee in the Lodge, where they had a generator. We used our fireplace and made beds on the floor in front of it. Shelters were opened in town, but animals had to be in a separate building. That was not a good idea for Daisy.

We drove to the next town to a restaurant that had a gas stove to buy some warm food. Very few gas stations were open, and of course, they were not receiving deliveries of gas. The police department offered the opportunity to charge cell phones, thank goodness! Although the sun appeared each day, it didn't help to melt the snow.

On the third day, we received a call from friends who lived in Woodbridge near New Haven. Woodbridge had electricity! "Please come to stay with us," said Susie. "Ed and I have been trying to get you. Come as soon as you can!"

It didn't take long for us to pack up and get on the road. It was forty-five minutes away, and we had enough gas. There was little traffic on the roads. Most people were huddled inside trying to stay warm.

"What would you like first—a glass of wine or a shower?" Susie asked when we arrived.

Ten minutes later, I was soaking wet and warm and clean ... pure heaven! (And then I had a glass of wine.) Daisy and Susie's dog Buddy had met and accepted each other. Tom unpacked and got his shower, and we shared stories from the past week with our friends.

Much of New Haven had electricity; the rest of the state did not and was hit very hard. Ed, Susie, and Buddy made us feel very welcome, but each day we called our place to check conditions. We didn't wish to overstay our welcome. After four days, we were told we could go back. We can never forget the kindness of dear Ed and Susie (and Buddy!).

★ ★ ★

Daisy lived with us another six months, and we never left her by herself again. No matter where we went, she went with us. Our community and our state recovered from the very harsh winter. We began to see a lot more of our neighbors and thought about entertaining once again because we loved to cook, and they all loved to eat. Daisy was always nearby and as sweet as ever, and we gave her all of our attention.

Spring arrived once again, and we were especially happy to see it. One day, we took out our beautiful Italian cookbook and called some good friends. Dinner was roasted beef with red wine, slow-baked for three hours, covered with sliced onions, basted with red wine, and then set at a higher temperature for the last hour. Conversation at the dining table was limited. Everyone was too busy eating. It was delicious!

Daisy lay on a couch nearby as the roast cooked. She hadn't eaten a lot lately but seemed OK otherwise. We had some meat left over, and I cut some bits for her. She went right to her dish and began to eat, but she didn't swallow the meat—just the juice. For three days, her diet was liquid. We went to Canton for advice, of course. Dr. Evans recommended putting her to sleep due to her inoperative digestive condition and her age. Another heartbreak!

We spent the next two days as close to her as we could be. On the morning of our appointment, I left her sleeping downstairs and went upstairs to fold laundry. As I peered over the railing, I saw Daisy standing at the bottom of the stairs looking up longingly toward the second floor. I hurried to finish my folding so that she wouldn't strain herself climbing the stairs, but before I could finish, she was at my side, panting from her climb. We sat on the floor together for a while, and I patted her soft back, and then it was time to go.

Dr. Evans came in to give her the first injection. "Dear Daisy, we love you. It's so hard not to cry!" When Dr. Evans returned with the second dose, Daisy struggled to stay alive. I don't remember our other hounds doing that. Our hearts were torn apart as we watched. She didn't want to leave us.

Daisy, the first time we met, you had to be coaxed out of a barn in Bethlehem. You became a lovely family member. You shared your space and your toys. You made us laugh and cry. We cherish every moment you gave us, dear Daisy!

Chapter 9

Sophie and Dora

On a sunny and warm afternoon, we pulled up to Eileen's garage in Bethany. We had called her the previous day to say we would be there to return Sophie and Dora.

"Is this a divorce?" Eileen exclaimed as we unloaded greyhound accessories from our car.

As we led Sophie and Dora, we explained, "We're sorry, we just can't manage these two! We're so sad, but they've driven us crazy, and we're exhausted!"

It was difficult to describe all that had happened in those three weeks. First of all, Sophie and Dora were straight off the track and had only been familiar with life in a kennel. At three in the morning, we were cleaning up our floors. If we couldn't go to the dog run, they wouldn't poop outside.

"The worst thing happened in Tom's office right after they finished breakfast one morning," I told Eileen. "Tom yelled, 'Stop!' but not in time to prevent Dora from biting off the end of Sophie's tail. I got the first aid kit and tried to clean and cover the wound as fast as possible. Sophie's tail never stopped wagging. I was covered with drops of blood. The walls outside of the office were splattered and reminded me of a Jackson Pollock creation, but only in red.

Next stop was Dr. Evans's office in Canton. By the time we arrived in an examining room, the bandage was off. Dr. Evans did the best he could to replace it with stronger coverings. Even then, Sophie continued to wag her tail.

With very little sleep, we faced each day with the intention of training them. What were we thinking when we decided on two dogs fresh from their racing careers? We had been fortunate with Ping and with Tootsie. They were quick studies. Celia had been totally house-trained, and Daisy quickly learned from Toots.

Tom and I were too old to handle this challenge. I spent hours scrubbing bloodstains from walls, carpeting, and my clothes. Dora seemed depressed much of the time, while Sophie seemed so happy all the time, just to be alive! We had to separate their eating areas and make sure they had no further altercations.

For three weeks, life with the girls was one huge chore. That's when we left Eileen the message that we would be returning them very soon.

It was awful to drive off without them and go back to an empty house. There hadn't been much time for fun, and we had hours of sleep to catch up on. We were sad and heartbroken.

For the next few weeks, I called Eileen or went to her REGAPCT website to check on the girls almost every day. A month later, she let us know that someone had adopted Dora and was getting her help for her depression. Soon after that, two sisters who had homes on the same street decided to share Sophie. They each had a fenced-in backyard where Sophie would be safe and happy. I'm sure her tail was still wagging.

What a relief it was to hear that good news! They were the best they could be at the time, and I'm sorry that we have no photos. They were beautiful girls.

Chapter 10

And Then Came Darby

Beloved by all

Each time one of our greyhounds passed, it took us time to recover. Life without them was no longer normal for us. The lesson we had learned from Sophie and Dora included the realization that we were not getting younger, and it was time to think about the future. Downsizing began to seem like a good idea. We put the house on the market and let all our friends and neighbors know that we were selling.

At a meeting one day, Tom found that one of the committee members was looking for a larger home with features similar to ours. His home was a better size for us, so we made a visit. Though he preferred to sell his home, he agreed to rent it to us while he bought ours. Perfect!

We needed to decide what would be best for the long term. Though we were without pets, we knew that we wanted others. The buyer (and prospective landlord) didn't want pets in his house but finally agreed to allow us one. The house he was buying had been home to five hounds over the years and was in mint condition.

In the few weeks before the closing, I checked Eileen's website each day for hounds available for adoption. I was drawn to one of the photos posted. It was a brindle female looking out a window through sheer curtains. Her name was Darby. Each day, I checked to see whether or not her photo remained. I began to feel as though Darby was waiting for me, and I called Eileen with questions.

Darby had been returned twice due to problems dealing with small children and other dogs, especially small ones. I was reminded of Celia and Daisy. Because we wanted to see more of Darby, we took a ride to Bethany.

Darby was in a shed with two hounds who were boarding. She lay in a corner looking forlorn. She didn't jump up to greet us, as most others would have done. When Eileen coaxed her over, she came and allowed me to greet and pet her. It made me sad that she seemed so sad. We had time to decide before we would be in our next home, and I wanted to be sure she would be OK by herself, since we would only be allowed one pet.

"Let us think about her and get back to you, Eileen. We have to move in a few weeks, so we'll wait until we're settled to bring another hound home. Darby might be happy with us, I think."

Would Darby be OK without a sister in the house? We would have lovely next-door neighbors in our new neighborhood, and they had a small black-and-white dog named Tuxedo. They spent winters in Florida and returned to Lakeridge in the spring. Could we cope with a dog next door? Could we hope to make Darby's life and our own happier? Darby was house-trained, neither a barker nor a whiner. We would make another visit to her soon.

The move went well. We would miss our house, but this one was cozy and had a room for Tom's office. The dog's loveseat/bed would fit into a corner of our bedroom. After a second trip to Eileen's, we decided to bring Darby home with us (with a muzzle, just in case). We had a month or so to wait before Carol, Spencer, and Tuxedo would be back from Florida. I was hopeful that we would work out any problems.

The first night I led her to her bed, Darby slept soundly. We waited a week before leaving her home alone for short periods of time. She seemed fine, but one day we left for a few hours and found a poop behind the front door upon our return. Darby was on the daybed in Tom's office. I leashed her for a walk and firmly told her that I was disappointed with what I had found and that we really wanted her to stay with us, but ...

Honestly, I think she understood me. We had no problems at all after that day. Darby soon became a best friend forever.

★ ★ ★

Winter had one more storm in store for us. On one April morning, the view through our picture window resembled a painting. A blanket of new-fallen snow had covered our neighborhood, and the morning sun studded the blanket with gleaming crystals.

Darby danced as I put on our warm coats and her leash. "Let's go, Darb!" I opened the storm door, and she lunged forward.

OMG! There were two young deer at the bottom of the steps, and their coloring matched Darby's. They stared at us for a moment, startled just as we were, and then scampered away to the woods, leaving a trail of their tracks in the snow. Darby whined briefly.

"Darby, they looked like your sisters!" I hugged her and took a breath of the cold fresh air, hoping that I would always remember what had happened on this beautiful morning.

It took a few days for that snow to begin melting. Usually, Tom took Darby out first thing in the morning while I made breakfast. On this particular day, they seemed to be out far too long. Breakfast was ready.

I grabbed my coat and boots but then heard clumping on the front steps. They were back.

"What happened?" I asked as Tom peeled off his snowy jacket and boots.

"It's icy because the streets were plowed. I slipped and fell down into a ditch. Luckily, Darby didn't slip with me. She just stood in place while I tried to climb out. I'm breathless, but not bruised! I'm cold and I'm hungry!"

I was sorry I hadn't been with them. I could have helped somehow. Enough of winter for this year!

A few days later, seven deer crossed the street right in front of them as Tom and Darby took their early-morning walk. From past experience, I guessed that they all lived near the top of the ski area, which was down the path from our house. Though they can be pesky, deer are very beautiful beings with gentle eyes and soft noses—so much like greyhounds.

Living in the woods of northwestern Connecticut, we often saw nature's creatures, including turkeys and rabbits. Once a mother bear and her two cubs crossed the road in front of our car as we climbed the hill to our home. Owls hooted at night while coyotes roamed below. Out at the stable, we had horses, chickens, goats, cats, and a pig. Dogs visited the run each day. It was wonderful!

★ ★ ★

Hooray! Carol and Spencer and Tuxedo were back. Spring was here! Carol came over to welcome us and to meet Darby. I explained Darby's

Unconditional

problem with little dogs, and we agreed to be cautious. Right away, Darby bonded with Carol, who had a wonderful way of speaking with dogs. We began to meet on the walkway outside our homes each day with our dogs on leashes. They did get used to each other.

Soon, Howard and Linda returned to their home a few doors away and invited all of us over for an afternoon. "Bring the dogs too," said Howard, and we did. He had bought a large bone for Darby and a small one for Tuxedo. Guess who grabbed the large one! Darby was content with the small one. We sat on the floor watching the dogs and exchanging funny stories. It was a special day and such a good time to be alive and well, and in each other's company.

★ ★ ★

Michael's art store was opening in town—a knitter's dream come true! In addition, the framing department was amazing. I applied for a sales position and was thrilled to join the framing department. As long as I was choosing matting and framing, I was really good. I even learned to cut glass and mats. I was not so great at measuring and ordering on the computer. However, I lasted a year as the oldest employee in the store. With all I had learned, I was able to frame a great photo I had taken of Tootsie and Daisy playing in a snow-covered dog run. I treasure it still.

Tom and I always enjoyed being active. Before my year at Michael's, we had volunteered at a Torrington elementary school. Eventually, we spent seven rewarding years working with the same wonderful teacher to help third- through fifth-grade students who were mainly from South and Central America with creative writing. We even brought Toots and Daisy to visit a few times. It was great to feel useful, and we loved the children and their stories.

Time has its way of moving on and taking us along for the ride. "What are we doing here?" Tom asked one day. "Our sons are in Los

Angeles and it's warm there. John loves to visit in winter for the snow, skiing, and hiking, but Tom Jr. can't get away from work too often." Though we loved New England very much, we were heading into our eighties and wanted to live closer to our boys.

Our lease would not be up for another year, but we began looking online for a senior living place in California. We had a wonderful friend and dog-sitter who stayed with Darby for a week, and off we flew to find a place not too far from LA. In Escondido in San Diego County, we found a residence with a pool and a lovely garden. We received permission to have a large dog living with us. It helped that she was a greyhound. It was a fairly long drive from Escondido to LA, but we didn't want to be too close and interfere with the boys' lives.

Our brokers found a person to take over our lease, and we began planning our move across the country. We had downsized two years before, but there was more to be done. We hired a person to help us sell what we no longer needed. Of course, we would so miss our friends and the four seasons, but reality had struck. It was time to make the choice about the move before others made it for us.

Chapter 11

Road Trip

Darby loved the car even more than her predecessors—perhaps because she didn't have to share the seat. Even though she was packed into the back seat of our Subaru with anything we couldn't fit into the trunk, she never complained. She was the best-behaved passenger we ever had. The moving van was on its way to the West Coast with several stops to make on the way and would meet up with us in Escondido the day after we arrived there.

The first morning, we left melting snow and reached snowless Fredericksburg, Virginia, by dinner time. It would be exciting to see my alma mater the next morning, probably for the last time—Mary Washington College, this time not as "a stranger in a strange land." Fond memories!

One last look, and we headed for Jacksonville, Florida, seven hundred miles away. It was dark when we arrived, and we were greeted warmly at our motel. We slept well, but we were concerned about all the signs on the lawn: "Beware of Alligators"!

Onward to Pensacola! It was hard to find our motel in the dark, but when we did, it was comfortable and had good TV, plus breakfast was free. What an amazing and very busy city!

Then, off we headed for Alabama and Mississippi. Crossing the Mississippi River on a beautiful sunny day was a thrill; seeing a chain gang of prisoners working on a road was not. In Alabama, we stopped for lunch. As we parked, a motorcycle carrying Santa, a reindeer, and a speaker playing Christmas music pulled up next to us. The two happily gave us directions to Route 10. We had been worried that we might run into problems with our "Yankee" license plates, but we never did.

Next was Baton Rouge, Louisiana, and then Beaumont, Texas, where our hotel, an Embassy Suites, featured glass elevators overlooking the lobby. Darby was terrified by this new experience. She had never ridden one of these. We almost had to carry her onto the elevator with us. Otherwise, it was a great stay. Before we left in the morning, we checked ahead to be sure our next hotel would accept dogs. We had reserved all stays in advance but always double--checked ahead of time. "Yes" was the answer.

It was dark when we reached the hotel in San Antonio. I went in to check in. It had taken us over an hour to find the hotel. We always tried to book places near the highways but were rarely successful. When Tom came in with Darby, the desk person said, "We don't allow dogs." I took a deep breath and related that we had called ahead and gotten a "yes." (At seven thirty at night, where else could we go?)

I asked to speak with a manager and pled our case. At first, the manager was unbending. Then I asked for a regional manager. We had used the same hotel chain for every stop we made and never had a problem before this. Finally, the local manager agreed to give us a back room with a door to the outside close by. She told us to say that Darby was a therapy dog if anyone asked. No one did. Whew!

Next day, we were happy to leave there. For lunch, we stopped at a Jack-in-the-Box along the way and noticed a light on our dashboard. Oil needed! We saw a garage directly across the street that specialized in oil changes—our good fortune. The couple who owned the station were lovely. They gave us a calendar for the new year, fussed over Darby, and made the time spent the best it could be.

New Mexico was next. On the way, we had a call from the movers to let us know they expected a certified check from us before they would unload our furniture in Escondido. We would have to find a Bank of America near Las Cruces.

The bank was easily found and very efficient and helpful. Our motel was comfortable. On our way to Arizona the next day, we saw herds of Black Angus cattle boarding trains. We didn't want to think about where they were going and didn't eat a hamburger for several weeks afterward.

Onward to the next Holiday Inn in Arizona. We were early and had some time to do laundry. There were two beautiful queen-size beds in our room, to Darby's delight. Tom got directions to an Olive Garden restaurant for our dinner, to his delight.

The restaurant was packed full, which was not a surprise. Tom decided to check out the bar. He came back to tell me that a young couple had offered to share their booth with us. They were delightful, as was the dinner, and Santa and Mrs. Claus were across from us sitting at the bar. In a week, they would be packing the sleigh for Christmas Eve. What fun!

The route into California had us passing through mountains covered with huge gray boulders, some so precariously perched on others that one could fear for one's life. There was not a trace of green in sight and very few cars on the well-paved and narrow two-lane road. We passed a border-guard station and saw a Mexican family, probably being detained. This was southern California, and there were no stops on the way through this area.

At long last, we reached San Diego and drove north toward Escondido. We phoned our new home, Westmont, for last-lap directions. In an hour, we were in the Westmont garage, arriving in the middle of a holiday party to which dogs were not invited. Helen, our new friend and marketing manager, brought us to our apartment, where we found refreshments and a welcome basket that included a bone for Darby. Right away, she found a soft corner of the carpet and lay down, as relieved as we were. Seven days of travel, and we were here at last. Tom and John would be here soon, and we'd have Christmas dinner together. Hooray!

The next day was Sunday, and my birthday. Our furniture arrived, and we settled with the movers. Dinner was a carving featuring a well-cooked roast of beef, and all the food was delicious. Our new life had begun.

How great to see Tom and John more often and to visit them in Los Angeles! We found a good dog sitter, a great veterinarian, and Petco for food and grooming. We made so many new friends, and Darby seemed thrilled with all the petting and treats she received.

★ ★ ★

One day we drove into the garage, and Tom asked me where we were. Tom's experience was diagnosed as a small stroke, which presented a challenge to our new lives. I had to become the driver in a state where a car was the primary mode of transportation. The streets and highways were always very busy. Somehow I managed to adjust and get us to and from offices nearby, where the health care has been the best.

In the meantime, after three wonderful years, Darby began to experience some health issues. She was almost fourteen and had become a cherished neighbor to the dog-lovers in our community. Many extra walks were needed, and accidents began to occur in the hallway. We made a number of trips to our very good vet, but Darby wasn't getting any better. I knew the end was near, and I took counsel with Irene, a new friend who had retired from a career as a therapist.

In life, one has to seek the greater good for all concerned. Never did I want a pet and family member to live in pain just for us. We had to do at least four walks each day, and Tom had mobility issues. So I became busier than ever. It was so difficult to think about, and it took many weeks of talks to plan to do what was merciful. After many tearful nights, we made an appointment.

A dear friend, Lorraine, drove Darby and me to a specialist who would put Darby to sleep. The office was very quiet, and we were ushered to an almost empty room where there was a blanket spread on the floor near a few chairs. I petted Darby and told her how much we loved her, what a wonderful girl she was, and that she would be all right. The doctor came and gave her the first shot, and soon she lay down on the blanket. I joined her on the floor and stroked her head and neck. Her ears were perked as she listened to me. Soon the doctor appeared to administer the second shot.

My last memory is of Darby looking at me with her ears still perked, listening to my every word as I told her how much we loved her. Her favorite toy was a teddy bear, which lies on our bed still. We couldn't have asked for a better companion for this time in our lives. We will always miss her terribly.

There was hardly a dry eye in the house for weeks after I posted a notice of Darby's passing at the lobby desk in our residence. I think of her and all our dear companions every day. If there is a heaven, greyhounds must be there, and I hope that I'll be there with them.

Chapter 12

More Change

LIFE WAS AS GOOD AS COULD BE UNTIL WE REALIZED THAT WE needed to modify our expenses. We looked for a place nearby so that we could keep in good touch with our friends in Escondido. A senior living community was the answer. As many have said, change is the order of life—and the changes are not always foreseen, perhaps because we don't want to see them.

Living with the reality of the coronavirus, and in this turbulent time of division in our country, is a challenge for everyone. I'm hopeful that with hard work, good will, and time, most of us will remember that we belong to each other. We are grateful for the wonderful lives we have had with our families, friends, kind strangers, and best friends: Ping Ping, Tootsie, Celia, Daisy, and Darby—and even Sophie and Dora. They enriched our lives and brought us both joy and sorrow. Without Eileen McCaughern, we might never have known the many wonderful moments we have experienced with our pets. We are better humans for having had them with us. Their love for us was truly unconditional, as ours was for them.

Chapter 13

Eileen

SMALL IN STATURE, EXTRA-LARGE IN SOUL, BLONDE AND BLUE-eyed, with a smile to melt your heart, Eileen McCaughern worked each week in the legal department of a large corporation. On weekends, she sold real estate. She did all of this in order to care for her REGAPCT hounds, oftentimes more than fifteen at a time, who needed forever homes. Eileen became a wonderful friend and told us her life story and gave us copies of so many articles about her life and life with her hounds.

As a child, Eileen had no pets. When she got to the University of Connecticut, she had saved enough to buy a horse and managed to start an equestrian program there. UConn has always had a very good agricultural department. It was a great place for Eileen to study. Consequently, she became such a good rider that she was offered a job as a jockey. She was excited about riding these beautiful animals. However, on the day of her first tryout, she fell from her horse and broke an arm. Her doctor recommended that she make another career choice.

Riding her horse through the New Hampshire woods one day following her graduation, Eileen saw a man walking a group of large dogs. "What breed are they?' she asked.

"Oh, they're greyhounds from the dog track, but their racing days are over. They and others will be destroyed."

Without hesitation, Eileen asked for one of the hounds. His name was Terry Canary, and she took him home with her to Bethany, Connecticut.

"From then on, I found all the information I could about racing greyhounds," she told me. "There were two tracks in Connecticut, and I lived near the one in Bridgeport. I found the vet who cared for the dogs there. He was a caring person and gave me lots of information. Rumor had it that the other track in another city was not as caring—the water was unclean along with the general environment. Dogs were moved in and out at all hours of the day and night. Something had to be done.

"I found friends, and we formed a rescue group and called ourselves REGAPCT—Retired Greyhounds as Pets, Connecticut. Word spread through the town and the state, and I was able to get support from veterinarians, pet stores, volunteers, school kids doing community projects for credit, and many others—and my second career began."

After being voted Pet Hero of the Year on the Animal Planet cable channel in 2008, Eileen built a small kennel in her large backyard and took in boarders to earn extra money. The award had included a trip to Ireland to visit greyhounds there along with a cash reward. Due to her hard work, at least five thousand greyhounds have been placed in forever homes. There are several very good interviews with Eileen on YouTube. She has been a wonderful friend to greyhounds.

One story worth telling starts with trucks and firefighters all over the street.

"OMG! OMG! My hounds, my house!" Eileen cried. "What happened? Did you get all the dogs? How about the birds?"

Eileen counted. *Two dogs are missing. They might be under the bed in my room!* "I must go in!" she told a firefighter.

"No, ma'am, we'll go in!" The brave man ran through the burning home and came out with two very frightened hounds. A second man retrieved the birds.

"Oh, thank goodness they are all safe! What happened?" Eileen asked.

"We think your house was struck by lightning," a firefighter replied. "One of your neighbors called us. The house is gone, but all the animals are safe."

"Thank you! Thank you! Thank you all!"

Within hours, most of Bethany came to the rescue with a trailer in which Eileen could live, as well as food and supplies for the dogs. Other greyhound rescue groups came to take a share of the dogs until rebuilding was complete. So many good friends, neighbors, animal lovers, and just plain good people appeared. It was July 8, 2008.

On this day, she had gone to an animal adoption meet to find a companion for a goose she had rescued. Sadly, an appropriate mate was not immediately available. So Eileen would try another time. Her reputation as an animal advocate had spread far and wide. At various times, she had housed a horse, ducks, and geese. Cats were not a good fit, and of course, rabbits were out of the question! However, her household included four birds in addition to the hounds.

The cause of the fire was found to be lightning striking an electrical connection in her sitting room where she and her birds would have been had she not been out looking for a gander. Saved not by the bell but a goose!

Thank goodness for first responders and all the heroes living and working in our world.

afterword

Greyhounds seem to have been highly regarded in Ancient Egypt. Their images have been found on the walls of pyramid tombs. Also, it is believed that they appeared in the Celtic area of Europe as early as 8 AD. Indeed, they may be the oldest purebred canine in history. Often they are found in paintings of the French courts and in art depicting the lives of titled English people. For a long time, only the wealthy were allowed to own them.

Because of their astute sense of sight (up to a thousand meters in distance), their intelligence, and their speed, greyhounds were used for hunting. Due to their gentle nature, they were also enjoyed as companions.

Over the years, they became an industry for Ireland, which began breeding and racing them and/or exporting them to the United States, Spain, and other countries, where they were not always treated well. Many groups and individuals have worked very hard to improve the lot of these lovely hounds. In fact, the dog-racing industry has lost much of its luster, and tracks in the United States are closing partially due to the work of the groups and to changing times.

In the beginning, tracks opened with the intention of simply exhibiting the amazing racing skills of the hounds. At first, live bait was used to lure the animals. The initial entry per person at one of these tracks was 99 cents. Grey2K USA Worldwide, organized to protect greyhounds, reports that Owen Patrick Smith of California, owner of the Blue Star Amusement Company, in the interest of being humane, then invented a mechanical lure fastened to the outside of the track. However, Mr. Smith did not foresee that greyhound racing would in many places become far less humane than was ever his intention.

An article published in *The Guardian*, a British newspaper, in November of 2018 and titled "The Slow Death of US Greyhound Racing" discusses Florida's vote to close tracks within the two years following the vote. As of December 2020, at least two tracks had closed.

What will become of this wonderful canine breed? Will their temperaments change when they no longer have training and experience racing before they are adopted? Or were they gentle and sweet from the beginning? We will know in time.

Many canines and other animals are mistreated and neglected in this country. There is always work to be done to address these problems. My hope is that there will always be people like Eileen and others who accept these challenges, and others who will support them.

about the author

Jeanne Cassidy was born in Brooklyn, New York, and lived on Long Island. After attending local schools, she chose Mary Washington College of the University of Virginia for her BA degree in Sociology. She and her husband, Tom, were married in 1957 and lived in Ridgefield, Connecticut, where they raised two sons. Jeanne taught in elementary schools there for twelve years, helping with curriculum writing. During that time, she earned two additional degrees in Education—one from Danbury State College and another from Fairfield University, both in Connecticut.

Always interested in the arts, Jeanne studied piano for many years and enjoyed writing for local community publications. Her second career was in the entertainment industry, working for MTV Networks and Viacom, where she headed the press library and edited a diversity newsletter. During that time, she was able to accompany her husband in business travel abroad.

Thanks to *The Joan Rivers Show*, she was inspired to adopt retired racing greyhounds, who became an important and wonderful part of her family life. In addition, writing became more and more interesting and enjoyable: mainly newsletters, poetry, and short stories. When taking care of pets became difficult, Jeanne chose to share the joy and love she had experienced with greyhounds in the hope that others would be inspired to consider them as pets—and so, this book.

Bibliography

Caldwell, Dave. "The Slow Death of US Greyhound Racing." *The Guardian* (November 20, 2018). https://www.theguardian.com/sport/2018/nov/20/the-slow-death-of-us-greyhound-racing-florida-ban.

Cassidy, Tom. "Special Feature: Greyhounds at Ground Zero—Tootsie's Odyssey." *CGMagazine* (Spring 2002). https://www.cgmagonline.com.

David Krechevsky. "Dogs Find Their Savior—Again." *Waterbury Republican American* (July 7, 2004).

Dog Daze of New Hartford. Brochure for the event created by the committee. October 2, 2005.

History.com Editors. "September 11 Attacks: How Many People Died in the 9/11 Attacks?"

McLoughlin, Pamela. "A Goose Saved Her Life, Bethany Animal Lover Says After House Fire." *New Haven Register* (July 7, 2004).

Pet Place Online (on Facebook; general information on pets and pet care). https://www.petplace.com.

Schenone, Laura. *The Dogs of Avalon*. New York: W.W. Norton & Company, 2017.